CONTENTS

EDITOR'S NOTES

In the fall of 1992, nearly 42 percent of all college and university faculty who were teaching courses for credit were employed part-time, and a growing percentage of full-time faculty (15 percent) were not eligible for tenure (Harper, 1998).

In this volume, the term *part-time faculty* will refer to individuals who are appointed to teach courses and who are employed on some basis other than a full-time contract. Sometimes referred to as *adjunct faculty,* whose employment is typically long term but part-time, this group also includes temporary hires who teach as substitutes, as fill-ins, or as on-call instructors and whose employment depends on adequate enrollment in courses. It does not refer to graduate teaching assistants or to faculty appointed to full-time positions without eligibility for tenure. The latter group are commonly referred to as *temporary faculty.*

Changes in Academic Work Patterns

Changes in the employment patterns of American academics—from a predominantly tenured or tenure-eligible faculty to a faculty more typically employed off the tenure track—appear to be joint products of several factors: supply-and-demand imbalances in the academic workforce, developing patterns of work and employment that are unique to individual academic disciplines, changes in the economic foundations and organization of American colleges and universities, and large underlying shifts in patterns of work in American society.

The causes and consequences of these trends were the subject of a seminar sponsored by the Alfred P. Sloan Foundation on December 2–3, 1997. Sloan Conference participants prepared analyses of these changes to address the following questions:

- Who are the new part-time, adjunct, and non-tenure-track faculty?
- What are the trends in academic careers?
- Are patterns of part-time work in academe similar to or different from the same patterns in other sectors?
- How does the economic condition of higher education affect the academic workforce?
- Is the use of part-timers and adjuncts supply-driven or demand-driven?

Source: Some of the data used in this volume are drawn from the National Center for Education Statistics' National Survey of Postsecondary Faculty (NSOPF), which was conducted in the fall of 1992. Respondents to the survey self-reported their full- or part-time status.

- Why do institutions elect to hire more part-time and adjunct faculty?
- What are the consequences for the production of knowledge and the quality of teaching?

A great deal is at stake in answering these questions, as well as in shaping the future of academic employment and the attractiveness and security of academic careers. At stake are the

- Continuity and progress in the production and application of knowledge
- Relative attractiveness of academic careers to talented people
- Quality and integrity of undergraduate and graduate education
- Ability of colleges and universities to respond to their changing environments
- Renewal of the nation's intellectual capital
- Nature and meaning of work and its relationship to the idea of careers in American culture

Is it really in the nation's interest to convert such a large proportion of academic jobs to temporary and short-term arrangements? The chapters in this volume were originally prepared for and presented at the Sloan Conference. Their collective goal is to explore the causes, effects, and implications of an increasingly temporary academic workforce, in particular, the rapidly expanding reliance on part-time and adjunct faculty.

Locations of Nontraditional Academic Employment

Where do the part-time and adjunct faculty teach and in what fields? Numbering over 376,000 (up from just over 250,000 in 1987), they teach in substantial numbers in all types of institutions (Kirshstein, Matheson, Jing, and Zimbler, 1997). Over 60 percent of faculty teaching courses at community colleges are part-time (Table 1). Research universities use proportionally far fewer part-time or adjunct faculty.

Table 1. Proportion of Part-Time Faculty by Institutional Type

Type of Institution	Part-Time	Full-Time
Research universities	23.4%	76.6%
Doctoral granting	32.2	67.8
Comprehensive universities	38.6	61.4
Private liberal arts colleges	35.5	64.6
Public two-year colleges	60.2	39.8
All other	48.3	51.7
Total all institutions	41.6	58.4

Source: National Center for Education Statistics, Survey of Postsecondary Faculty, 1993.

The individual disciplines also use part-time and adjunct faculty in different proportions, as Ernst Benjamin's reports in Chapter Five. In some fields more than half of all faculty are part-timers; in others, fewer than one-quarter are.

Differences Between Part-Time Faculty and Full-Time Faculty

Part-time faculty resemble full-time faculty more closely than is commonly supposed. Most have middle-class incomes; they have families, and, perhaps surprisingly, they have well-paying, full-time jobs. Other characteristics are as follows:

Almost two-thirds (63.7 percent) reported that they held full-time jobs elsewhere while teaching part-time.

Mean household income of part-time faculty was $67,637, compared to $81,248 for full-time faculty. Individual part-time faculty were the principal income producers in their households, averaging $48,743 in total *individual income* from all sources. (Their pay from their teaching jobs averaged $10,180 per year.)

Part-time faculty have held their present teaching positions for an average of 6.3 years (versus 11.2 years for full-time faculty).

Part-time faculty did differ from full-time faculty in two important respects. Most part-timers held a master's degree or less; only about 15 percent held the doctorate, and another 11 percent held the first-professional degree. Also, nearly half of all women faculty were part-time, whereas close to two-thirds of male faculty were full-time.

The majority of part-time and adjunct faculty (52 percent) reported that they prefer part-time teaching. A smaller proportion (43 percent) reported that they were teaching part-time because full-time jobs were not available.

Reasons for More Part-Time and Adjunct Faculty

The rise in numbers of part-time faculty has paralleled a rise in production of doctorates. Although oversupply of doctorally prepared prospective faculty may account for some of the heavy reliance on part-time faculty, oversupply appears to be only one factor—and then only in some fields, such as the humanities.

The increasing enrollment and numbers of program offerings in community colleges appear to have been the most important factors behind the rise in part-time faculty. "Over all, from 1970 to 1995, the number of faculty members at two-year institutions grew by 210 per cent, compared with 69 per cent at four-year institutions" (Schneider, 1998). Twenty years ago, just over one-half of all community college faculty were part-time; that figure had risen to

60 percent by 1992. As many as 80 percent of teaching faculty at some community colleges are part-time (Slingo, 1998).

The rise also paralleled the dramatic leveling off of state support for higher education in the early 1990s. Two of the chapters that follow in this volume (Chapters Eight and Nine) suggest that increasing enrollment and static revenue were important factors in reallocating faculty positions from full-time to part-time.

Has aging and the commensurate "tenuring in" of full-time faculty contributed to the hiring of more part-timers? Although institutions may be making long-term calculations about effects of the uncapped retirement age, the data from the 1992 survey did not indicate that this was an immediate or even a short-term crisis that might explain the relatively rapid increase in employment of part-time faculty (see also Baldwin and Chronister, 1996).

Is the increasing use of part-time faculty connected to the shifting of full-time faculty effort away from undergraduate instruction? NSOPF data show that full-time faculty, on the average, taught three courses per semester—mostly undergraduate courses—and generated more student credit hours per course taught (104.7) than part-time faculty did (77.4). Sloan Seminar participants did suggest that part-time faculty may be hired to help absorb increasing enrollments or to help develop new or changing programs. But there is no compelling evidence that full-time faculty have diverted their efforts from undergraduate instruction.

The changing gender composition of the professoriate is sometimes offered as an explanation. However, the data suggest that women do not prefer part-time work arrangements more than men do. Just over half of both genders preferred part-time work; 52.9 percent of male part-timers preferred it, as did 51.3 percent of female part-timers.

Undoubtedly, *there is no single, simple explanation for the increase in the number of part-time and adjunct faculty in American colleges and universities.* It is clear that this rise is not uniform across all sectors of higher education—patterns of faculty employment seem to be different in each sector. Also, the various academic disciplines act as somewhat unique labor markets, affected in different ways by changing enrollments, doctoral pipeline patterns, the shifting emphasis on program content, and many other issues.

When all of this evidence is boiled down, it appears that two other overriding factors stand out: (1) community colleges have expanded rapidly and have employed large numbers of part-time and adjunct faculty to staff that expansion, and (2) financial hard times and increased competition have forced colleges and universities to hedge on their commitments to long-term employment of full-time, tenure-track faculty.

Attitudes of Part-Time Faculty

The global picture of part-time faculty attitudes is one of competence, high morale, and a healthy level of professional engagement. But pockets of discontent exist. The attitudes of part-time faculty who report that they cannot find full-time work show the highest levels of dissatisfaction. In fine arts, 65 percent of the part-time faculty reported that full-time work was not available, and in the humanities 61 percent did. These are far higher percentages than in other fields. Part-time faculty in these two fields, and for whom full-time work was unavailable, expressed higher levels of dissatisfaction with their jobs "overall" than faculty similarly situated in other fields (32.2 percent in the humanities reported overall dissatisfaction; 27 percent of those in fine arts also reported dissatisfaction).

Organization of the Book

The purpose of the Sloan Conference was exploratory. Participants brought an array of perspectives, both theoretical and practical, to the discussion. In this volume, Fred Jacobs sets the stage for discussion with an analysis of decisions about faculty staffing facing one institution and how those decisions have led to hiring more part-time faculty. Chapters Two and Three put part-time academic work in context. Janet H. Lawrence lays out a conceptual framework for understanding academic careers and suggests that an increasingly contingent workforce would modify how faculty grow, develop, and master the basic elements of job and career. M. Edith Rasell and Eileen Appelbaum examine trends toward contingent work in the broader economy and look at the probable parallels in the academic arena.

Chapters Four and Five examine the basic questions, Who teaches part-time, where do they teach, and why? Donald N. Langenberg (in Chapter Four) surveys the many different categories of appointments among those who teach and do research in American colleges and universities. Although part-time faculty may constitute one growing subgroup among those who teach undergraduates, Langenberg reminds the reader that subfaculty in many different kinds of positions have gradually taken on the increasingly differentiated and complex functions of research universities. Ernst Benjamin (in Chapter Five) analyzes variations in characteristics of part-time faculty by teaching field. His analysis focuses on the differences between part-timers in traditional arts and sciences disciplines and those teaching in vocational and professional areas. He suggests that conditions for the two groups are substantially different, noting that vocational and professional part-timers are more likely to be voluntary and that liberal arts part-timers are more likely to feel constrained and economically vulnerable.

Chapters Six and Seven explore the institutional and organizational consequences of changing patterns of academic work. Catherine D. Gaddy (in Chapter Six) discusses the implications of emerging patterns of academic employment for knowledge production and careers in science. She focuses particularly on recommendations to mitigate the pitfalls of part-time jobs—for individuals, as well as for institutions and the scientific enterprise at large. In Chapter Seven, Pamela S. Tolbert reports that the use of part-time faculty in one department at a research university ultimately led to a separation of the two faculties into two departments, each with distinct goals. Specialization of work largely coincided with faculty status: part-timers typically taught language classes, whereas full-timers taught literature and linguistics. Work and status differences eventually led to splitting the department. Tolbert analyzes both antecedent organizational conditions and consequences, and she offers recommendations for policy and practice.

Chapters Eight and Nine report on the use of part-time faculty in a large suburban community college and a public comprehensive university. Chapter Ten discusses implications for policy, practice, and research. These cases illustrate common factors (for example, financial and enrollment pressures) and important differences (for example, market factors affecting the availability of qualified faculty) among institutions that suggest more particular attention to program and institutional goals as a framework for analyzing the use of part-time faculty. Finally, Chapter Eleven focuses on implications for further research, for policy, and for practice.

Conclusion

Part-time and non-tenure-track faculty now constitute a majority of all who teach in the nation's colleges and universities. The proportion of these nontraditional faculty appears to be far greater than workers in nonstandard arrangements in other sectors of the economy, marking higher education as an anomalous case. A large share of the escalating numbers of part-timers can be traced to increased staffing in community colleges and to financial pressures to control the cost of salaries and benefits for full-time faculty.

But the Sloan Conference participants made it abundantly clear that the effectiveness and validity of the whole higher education enterprise is entangled in the question of what faculty do, how their work and careers are constructed, and whether they can achieve the ends that society wants from its colleges and universities. It is not necessarily clear that one system—the traditional tenure track—is best. Neither is it clear that the path toward an increasingly temporary and contingent faculty is necessarily better. This volume is intended to provoke further study of how the most talented and committed people can be most fruitfully engaged in academic work and what arrangements of opportunity might best serve both the aspirations of those individuals and the needs of society.

References

Baldwin, R. G., and Chronister, J. L. *Full-Time Non-Tenure-Track Faculty*. Washington, D.C.: National Education Association Research Center Update (vol. 2, no. 5), Sept. 1996.

Harper, E. P. "A Study of Full-Time Non-tenure-track Faculty in Higher Education." Charlottesville: Center for the Study of Higher Education, Curry School of Education, University of Virginia, 1998.

Kirshstein, R. J., Matheson, N. J., Jing, Z., and Zimbler, L. J. *Instructional Faculty and Staff in Higher Education Institutions: Fall 1987 and Fall 1992*. Washington, D.C., U.S. Government Printing Office, 1997.

Schneider, A. "More Professors Are Working Part Time, and More Teach at 2-Year Colleges." *Chronicle of Higher Education,* Mar. 13, 1998. (http:\\www.chronicle.com)

Slingo, J. "2-Year College in Texas to Hire 60 Full-Time Professors. *Chronicle of Higher Education,* Feb. 20, 1998. (http://www.chronicle.com)

David W. Leslie
Editor

DAVID W. LESLIE is professor of education at the College of William and Mary in Williamsburg, Virginia.

Pragmatic and strategic practices can be used to "fix" some of the deficits identified in the use of part-time faculty.

Using Part-Time Faculty More Effectively

Frederic Jacobs

I am often told that administrative decisions about part-time faculty are ad hoc, resource-driven, and shortsighted. "Why," I am asked, "can't administrators make decisions and policies about part-time faculty that are more effective, more consistent, and more beneficial to the learning process?"

Taking as axiomatic that most academic administrators would prefer to strengthen rather than weaken the quality of instruction (an assertion some would challenge), why do the problems concerning part-time faculty appear so intransigent? It isn't for lack of trying or for failing to understand the problems; it isn't ignorance of strategies and approaches in use elsewhere; and it isn't just resource constraints. So what is it, exactly? I will try to answer some of these questions in this chapter.

For seven years, while serving as dean of faculties at American University, I was responsible for making policy recommendations to the provost and the university senate regarding part-time faculty. This chapter draws on my experiences and reflections and on problems and practices reported to me by colleagues at other institutions.

I suggest that policies related to part-time faculty all too often pursue consistency and regularity when the problems those policies are addressing are rooted in inconsistency and irregularity. My major premise is that better policy and improved practice would result if they were based on conscious disaggregation of the circumstances under which part-time faculty are hired and under which they work.

Virtually every academic administrator who deals consistently with issues related to part-time faculty asserts that there are good and bad reasons for using part-time faculty and that the bad reasons emerge from constraints such as economics, personnel, and time. If more funds were available, according to conventional wisdom, the problems would disappear. If there could be more lead time between registration and the start of classes. . . . There are many such "if's."

But in the sobering days of the 1990s, even this recovering administrator can see the stark reality that those constraining issues are not transient; they are permanent and there will never be enough money, time, or personnel to eliminate the problems caused by scarce resources. An examination of part-time faculty members' status, their working conditions, and their role in instructional delivery indicates that the problems associated with their increased involvement are of long standing and sometimes appear to be intractable. Numerous studies have focused attention on these issues, proposing a variety of strategies for amelioration (Gappa, 1984; Gappa and Leslie, 1993; Leslie, Kellams, and Gunne, 1982).

Administrators, therefore, must contend with the bad reasons—how to ameliorate them and how to make the best of a tough situation. Not a single administrator—whether in casual talk among peers, in discussions of research and exemplary programs, in the accreditation process, in the creation of institutional mission statements and strategic plans—not a one predicts the elimination of the problems related to the excessive use of part-time faculty, either for the short or the long term.

It would be easy in these circumstances to bemoan the status quo, but more constructive things can be done. First, administrators can note the limited circumstances in which the use of part-time faculty is beneficial and attractive and separate those uses from the more expedient ones. Second, administrators can disaggregate the various uses of part-time faculty and tailor policies to fit particular programmatic needs. Finally, administrators can work to include part-time faculty in the institutional culture by defining roles, creating norms, and sharing values and symbols. The power of inclusion in the culture has been underestimated and undervalued, and even though it affords few real solutions, inclusion does raise morale and engage the commitment of part-time faculty to quality.

This chapter explores three areas: (1) factors influencing the hiring of part-time faculty, (2) problems emerging from part-time appointments, and (3) policy and structural changes to increase effectiveness of part-time faculty.

Factors Influencing the Hiring of Part-Time Faculty

The tradition of part-time faculty in colleges and universities was firmly established long before the modern era. First, from the late Middle Ages onward, it was an ecclesiastical tradition to send priest-scholars to different universities to pursue their scholarly interests and to work with others. From the nineteenth century onward, this tradition was evident in American colleges and universities as they designated a "visiting" status to ministers and scholars from other institutions. Second, as medical and other professional schools developed in the post-Civil War period, practitioners were often invited to join institutions in a part-time clinical capacity. Finally, for much of the twentieth century, individuals in the public eye, including creative artists and public officials, have been sought after as "in-residence" faculty.

These three categories—visiting, clinical, and in-residence—include some of the most creative and effective uses of part-time faculty. In every sense the arrangements are mutually beneficial. The institutions benefit from having practitioners who bring their knowledge and skill to the classrooms and laboratories, while the practitioners have access to resources and a forum in which their work can be pursued and their ideas expressed. This was the framework for part-time appointments for decades, and the appointment process tended to be both informal and ad hoc. This framework serves two important institutional objectives: part-time faculty (1) enhance institutional prestige by bringing to the institution those with talent and reputation and (2) provide opportunities to make individuals available who have unique abilities or achievements in areas not represented by the full-time faculty.

Many of the country's leading institutions have prestigious visiting and in-residence programs, providing opportunities for part-time affiliation, sometimes on a short-term basis, occasionally for extended periods of time. In some institutions, the appeal of diversity and the potential to attract a prominent person for a short period of time has led to the reallocation of funding from a full-time faculty position to support these types of appointments.

The appointment of clinicians also serves these objectives. Particularly in medical schools but in other professional schools as well, clinical faculty appointments link the training functions of universities to the world of practice. In virtually all medical schools, part-time clinical appointments far outnumber the full-time faculty, sometimes by a factor of five or six.

These appointments constituted the majority of part-time faculty until after World War II, when the dramatic expansion of American higher education made it imperative to increase the use of part-time faculty. If the earlier history of part-time appointments was related to enhancing prestige and providing instruction in specialized areas, the more recent history has been dominated by enrollment fluctuations and managerial and financial imperatives. In the peak years of baby-boom enrollments, the use of part-time faculty increased considerably, reaching 22 percent in 1970 (National Center for Education Statistics, 1997). That increase represented one component of the overall hiring pattern that began emerging at the time; another component has been the gradual decline in the number of tenure-track faculty positions available (see Chapter Five). The final component has been the dramatic increase in the use of graduate assistants as part-time faculty members in baccalaureate institutions (Statement, 1997).

The current environment is more complex, and the most common reasons institutions use part-time faculty are illustrated in Table 1.1.

In this more recent context, the rationale for part-time faculty appointments has shifted dramatically from the need for specialists (visiting, clinical, and in-residence appointments) to the expedient need for temporary instructional assistance.

The need for temporary assistance emerges both from internal and external factors. Internally, institutions need temporary help when faculty members are on leave, are ill, or depart abruptly; they need help to fill in "gaps" when

Table 1.1. Differential Uses of Part-Time Faculty

Need	Explanation	Strategies for Consideration
Teaching multisection courses	In required introductory courses such as writing, foreign languages, and mathematics, more sections are needed than can be taught by "permanent" faculty.	Offer multiyear contracts and flexible arrangements to move from part-time to full-time status as institutional needs dictate.
Temporary replacements	Sudden changes in faculty status or circumstances may create a temporary vacancy.	Establish preference system to offer opportunities to currently serving part-time faculty.
Unanticipated enrollments	With enrollment fluctuations, there may be the need to teach some courses on relatively short notice.	Establish an incremental salary structure so that part-time faculty are paid more each semester they teach a particular course, with a special supplement paid for late notification to teach.
Clinical and other supervision	Programs such as student teaching, internships, and independent study require labor-intensive work, often in the field.	Create a category of part-time faculty who can serve as "clinical supervisors"

there are no full-time faculty with instructional expertise in particular areas. Most significantly, they need help when enrollments exceed projections. External factors affect enrollment and the need for instructional faculty; changes in the economy and changes in the availability of loans and grants affect enrollment; and changes in the job market affect the choice of majors and the demand for particular courses.

Fiscal considerations are primary. It is cheaper to hire part-time faculty than full-time faculty; it entails less of a commitment to hire temporary rather than tenure-track, tenured, or even long-term contract faculty. Both public and private institutions, faced with increased costs and increased public criticism of high tuition, view the hiring of part-time faculty as one source of flexibility in budgets dominated by fixed costs. Budget flexibility is an important goal of administrators, and the increased use of part-time faculty is one way to achieve it (Rhoades, 1996). Taken together, these factors have resulted in a significant increase in the use of part-time faculty; recent data from the National Survey of Postsecondary Faculty (National Center for Education Statistics, 1997) indicate that 42 percent of all instructional faculty are employed part-time.

But budget flexibility may be achieved at the cost of exploiting part-time faculty, who work with little or no job security, low wages, few benefits, and lack of opportunity for professional development or advancement. Part-time faculty, as a result, are often dissatisfied with their terms of employment, and administrators are dissatisfied with the inefficiencies and exigencies of a system that does not enable planning, evaluation, and quality control to occur consistently and systematically.

Because these constraints will likely continue over the next decades, administrators will remain challenged to find better ways to improve terms of employment and working conditions for part-time faculty. Three strategies are likely to assist in achieving this: (1) improving appointment, evaluation, and retention procedures, (2) disaggregating the roles and circumstances for which part-time faculty are used, and (3) creating opportunities to enable part-time faculty to become engaged with the institutional values and culture.

Problems Emerging from Part-Time Appointments

Institutional and individual problems are associated with part-time appointments, and each affects the other (Biles and Tuckman, 1986). Because so many decisions to hire are made in response to changed circumstances—sudden surges in enrollment or full-time faculty departures—the decision-making process is seldom as orderly or comprehensive as might be desired. In fact, at many institutions more than two-thirds of the appointments made for any semester are made in the thirty days preceding the start of the semester; in one regional survey several years ago, 10 percent of part-time appointments were made after the start of classes.

What are the implications of this from an institutional perspective? Decisions are hastily made, and the criteria for selection are dominated by availability and willingness to accept an offer. The quality of prior teaching experience may be a secondary consideration.

One example of the compromises created by quick decisions is illustrative. In an effort to upgrade the quality of part-time appointments, an institution enacts a policy requiring that part-time faculty who have previously taught at the institution have prior teaching evaluations included in the appointment request. Because the teaching evaluations are maintained by departments and may be difficult to locate, some evaluations may not be located until weeks after the semester has begun. In such instances, administrators are faced with a choice between ignoring the requirement and not appointing someone who may have a proven track record but no documentation.

Central administrators are not the only administrators challenged by the need to make decisions on short notice. Department chairs are reluctant to say they have no back-up part-timers, and they rely heavily on word of mouth to identify potential part-time faculty. At department meetings early in the semester, it is a telltale sign if the department chair is meeting part-time faculty members for the first time.

Another institutional dilemma arises when there are multiple sections of the same course—some taught by full-time and some by part-time faculty. Typically, full-time faculty are more accessible to students, have offices and office hours, are familiar with the institutional services available to students, and have an understanding of grading and performance norms for the courses they teach. In most institutions, part-time faculty are not required to meet individually with students or to have scheduled office hours; frequently they are not assigned an office or a campus telephone number. This means that students can have significantly different educational experiences, particularly in regard to their access to faculty members, based on arbitrary scheduling decisions. This puts some students at a disadvantage and creates an inconsistency of standards for (and services to) all students.

When hired under such conditions, part-time faculty experience ambivalence, conflict, and frustration about the circumstances under which they were hired. At a voluntary meeting at the end of one semester, part-time faculty were asked for suggestions about how their experiences could be made more successful and their teaching performances improved. Fully half of them indicated that the lack of time to prepare adequately was a major problem.

Research data indicate that the majority of those teaching on a part-time basis were initially seeking other employment (frequently full-time teaching) and that a significant number are also teaching at other institutions (Leslie, 1989). This means that within the cadre of part-time faculty there is a prevailing sense that teaching part-time is an alternative—not a primary choice. It also means that part-time faculty with commitments to more than one institution may use generic rather than institution-specific syllabi. In some institutions, where there is relative stability in the part-time faculty, as many as two-thirds of the faculty each semester have taught in the preceding one. That means, however, that in any semester, one-third of the part-time faculty are new. In institutions with less stability for part-time faculty, the percentage of new faculty may be much higher.

The problems facing these part-time faculty are formidable: little if any time to prepare in advance of the semester, little or no institutional knowledge, pressure from having multiple commitments, and a fundamental preference to have different employment.

Institutional administrators are often expected to justify the inequities and inconsistencies of this amalgam of policies and practices to students and parents, as well as to legislators and trustees. The problems are complex and so are explanations. A variety of institutional circumstances converge, and the quick fix is often to use part-time faculty. But there is no quick fix. The problems emerge from many sources, and the solutions require many strategies. Efforts to apply consistent policies to all circumstances involving part-time faculty may exacerbate the underlying problems. A more practical approach may involve a multifaceted strategy based on programmatic exigencies and priorities. Uniformity of practice, insofar as part-time faculty are concerned, may be administratively efficient but educationally unsound.

Sometimes, relatively simple solutions to complex problems can be formulated. Although there are significant systemic issues in how part-time faculty are used in higher education institutions, some low- or no-cost strategies could improve efficiency and effectiveness. Some of these suggestions are indicated in Table 1.2.

Table 1.2. Low- or No-Cost Strategies to Enhance Efficiency and Effectiveness

Locus of Initiative	Type of Cost	Strategies for Consideration
Institutional		
	None	Establish policies to create multiyear appointments (defined as eligibility to teach) to expedite the appointments process.
	One-time cost for professional preparation and modest costs for annual updating and printing	Prepare and publish a *Handbook* for part-time faculty indicating resources and services available to students so part-time faculty can be well informed and helpful to students.
	Variable, depending on available resources and facilities	Make part-time faculty accessible to students, providing offices, voice mail, e-mail, mailboxes.
	None	Add part-time faculty to institution mailing lists; provide accesss to services such as library and computer center.
	None, with minimal risk of some contingent costs in future semesters	Guarantee a minimum number of courses to be taught over a multiple semester period (for example, four courses over six semesters).
College or School		
	None, with minimal risk of some contingent costs in future semesters	Offer provisional contracts up to thirty days prior to the start of a semester, paying an amount equal to __% of the total amount if the course is later canceled.
	None, except the cost of updating and printing	Provide an "environmental scan" that describes norms, contexts, and standards for the college or school and department.
Academic Department		
	Time of faculty members	Provide feedback on performance, based on student evaluation of teaching data and observation of teaching by full-time faculty members.
	Clerical support	Provide logistical support to order books, type syllabi and assignments, arrange for special equipment needs, and so forth.
	None	If last-minute appointments (less than thirty days before the semester begins) are necessary, give preference to those already scheduled to teach or to those who have previously taught.

To this list, one of George Orwell's (1968) rules for effective communication must be added: "Break any of these rules sooner than say anything outright barbarous".

Changes to Increase Effectiveness of Part-Time Faculty

If administrators can separate out the circumstances in which part-time faculty are employed, more tailored approaches can be formulated and implemented. Administrators can, in fact, increase their own flexibility by finding ways to create category-specific policies for part-time faculty. By addressing the requirements of these differentiated teaching and instructional roles, it may be possible to recruit and retain a part-time faculty whose qualifications and interests are more aligned with the particular objectives of programs (Biles and Tuckman, 1986).

Ultimately, the major obstacle to establishing more effective institutional policies and practices for part-timers is budgetary. As the availability of full-time positions becomes less fluid, the pool of those willing to work as part-time faculty gets larger, and "institutions faced with budget limitations find part-time and adjunct faculty appointments irresistibly cost effective" (Statement, 1997, p. 5). While the statement goes on to note that "the immediate cost savings that institutions realize from widespread use of part-time appointments . . . are often offset by the lack of program coherence and reduced [full-time] faculty involvement with students and student learning" (p. 6), institutions are impelled by the need for balancing budgets and constraining costs. In such an environment, perhaps the most effective short-term strategies are those aimed at improving the circumstances in which part-time faculty members work. Realistically, if institutions cannot provide the fundamental changes some part-time faculty advocate, then, at a minimum, they should endeavor to reduce dissatisfaction and dysfunction.

Conclusion

In the end, part-time faculty dissatisfaction can be generalized as falling into two areas: work conditions and institutional culture. Low salaries, little job security, no office, no telephone—all are components of the dismal work conditions many part-time faculty describe. Whether these can be remedied is a function of institutional resources and administrative will. The need for change is obvious, but there is little agreement on how to achieve change. Efforts to improve work conditions through salary increases, benefits, and limited job security or assurance of continuity of service may yield some results. But if money is unavailable to hire full-time temporary or tenure-track faculty, it is unrealistic to believe that it can be made available to all part-time faculty. Although many administrators acknowledge the defects of present practice, they also recognize the budgetary flexibility afforded them by present practice.

The future is likely to be a continuation of the present. Incremental changes may occur. Indeed, budgetary flexibility may increase, either as a consequence of the current debates about tenure or as a result of the predicted baby-boom faculty retirements. But the issues and problems resulting from the use of part-time faculty will remain. What else can be done? Given the constraints, can the problems be fixed? The administrator's response—predictably and inevitably—is, it depends. Yes, the problems can be reframed and reconfigured; no, they cannot be resolved to everyone's satisfaction. The best prospects are to continue to whittle away at issues surrounding work conditions and to focus on institutional culture.

Institutional culture can be a vehicle for improving satisfaction and productivity. Part-time faculty can be helped to be more effective in their work if they understand the values and norms of the institution. It is not that part-time faculty should be made part of the culture because it would make them feel good; rather, they need to be included so they can understand what is valued, what is expected, and what they should value and expect. A culture of separation, in which part-time and full-time faculty describe themselves differently to students ("I have no office hours" and "I have no phone on campus") creates inequities for students and injures the institution. There are high- and low-cost items in the institutional culture, and there are tangible and intangible components as well. Establishing an inclusive culture does not necessarily imply significant expenditures; it does imply significant effort, but it is an effort worth undertaking.

What are the elements involved in creating an institutional culture that would enhance the experiences of part-time faculty? Initiatives from the top down are important; inclusion at the departmental level is significant; a hot line to get questions answered and problems resolved is helpful; a mentoring system for first-time part-timers can be effective; an end-of-semester debriefing can be beneficial. Although offices, telephones, and perks can make the part-time faculty member's experience more enjoyable, the benefits of inclusion in the culture can make it more satisfying and rewarding, both to the part-time faculty and to those they teach.

References

Biles, G. E., and Tuckman, H. P. *Part-Time Faculty Personnel Management Policies.* New York: American Council on Education/Macmillan, 1986.

Gappa, J. M. *Part-Time Faculty: Higher Education at a Crossroads.* ASHE-ERIC Higher Education Research Report no. 3. Washington, D.C., 1984.

Gappa, J. M., and Leslie, D. W. *The Invisible Faculty: Improving the Status of Part-Timers in Higher Education.* San Francisco: Jossey-Bass, 1993.

Leslie, D. W., Kellams, S. E., and Gunne, G. M. *Part-Time Faculty in American Higher Education.* New York: Praeger, 1982.

Leslie, D. W. "Creative Staffing: Problems and Opportunities." In G. G. Lozier, and M. J. Dooris (eds.), *Managing Faculty Resources.* New Directions for Institutional Research, no. 63. San Francisco, Jossey-Bass, 1989.

National Center for Education Statistics. *Instructional Faculty and Staff in Higher Education Institutions: Fall 1987 and Fall 1992.* Washington, D.C.: National Center for Education Statistics, 1997.

Orwell, S., and Angus, I. *The Collected Essays, Journalism, and Letters of George Orwell,* Vol. 4. London: Secker & Warburg, 1968.

Rhoades, G. "Reorganizing the Faculty Workforce for Flexibility." *Journal of Higher Education,* 1996, *67,* 629–659.

"Statement on the Growing Use of Part-Time and Adjunct Faculty." Statement issued by Ten Learned Societies and Faculty Associations, Washington, D.C., Dec. 1997.

FREDERIC JACOBS is professor of education and director of the doctoral program in the School of Education at American University, Washington, D.C.

Changes in academic careers call for a reexamination of the elements of academic work and their relationships.

A Framework for Assessing Trends in Academic Careers

Janet H. Lawrence

Readers interested in the study of academic careers can find a substantial array of research articles and essays in which the behaviors, beliefs, values, perceptions, and productivity of faculty are portrayed. The empirical work encompasses a range of approaches from the study of individuals in single institutions (Tierney, 1997) to national surveys (Blackburn and Lawrence, 1995; Fairweather, 1996; Gappa and Leslie, 1993).

This variety of approaches provides a rich literature but makes generalizing about academic careers very challenging. So in this chapter, I propose a way to frame our conversations about academic careers and illustrate how the framework may help us categorize the findings from different studies. I then suggest how modifications in graduate education and employment practices may affect different aspects of academic careers, giving particular attention to the use of part-time and adjunct faculty.

Theoretical Dimensions of Academic Careers

As I reflected on my campus experiences and on my reading, I realized that I had to distinguish among several concepts: *career, career course, role, work pattern,* and *workforce.* I took *career* to be the set of hierarchically ordered and professionally relevant positions within a field or discipline in which entrance and progression are regulated by peers. The *career course* is distinguished from *career* in that it refers to the configuration of activities and positions that characterize an individual within a field or profession—the way his or her work life manifests itself over time. *Role,* in contrast, is the set of responsibilities and rights one assumes when occupying a particular career-related position, for example, the faculty role within a particular type of college or university, a particular department, and so forth. *Work pattern* is how one carries out these role-related responsibilities and how one exercises these rights. The *workforce* refers to the people employed in a profession at a particular time—a collective that can be subdivided into groups by ascribed and achieved characteristics, for example, women, racial groups, graduate cohorts, professorial rank, and discipline.

Some refinements in my thinking were prompted by writers and researchers such as Finkelstein (1984), who distinguishes the structural from the normative aspects of faculty roles and careers. The structural aspects of roles are the constraints on one's activities (for example, assigned activities and available resources). The normative aspects are the felt pressures or prescriptions regarding role activities, that is, which ones are most and least valued or how one ought to carry out a particular responsibility.

The structural features of academic careers are as follows: (1) the delineation of employment tracks (for example, tenure-track faculty, research scientists, and administrators); (2) the stipulation of the sequencing of positions along a particular track (for example, academic ranks and the administrative bureaucracy); and (3) the regulation of access and movement (for example, the availability of faculty positions and contractual arrangements regulating periods of appointment and reappointment).

The normative features include (1) felt pressure to make certain career decisions (for example, graduates of research universities may be urged to seek faculty positions in particular types of institutions) or the attractiveness of alternative career tracks (for example, relative valuations of tenure-track, non-tenure-track, and administrative paths); (2) the institutional and disciplinary legitimacy of different tracks (for example, the governance rights accorded to part-time and adjunct faculty); and (3) the expectations that regulate access to and movement along tracks (for example, credentials for initial appointment and performance criteria for promotion that reflect institutional values). Some norms are expressed directly, whereas others are tacit (Tierney, 1997). Faculty learn what is expected of them through social interactions and vicarious experiences.

These distinctions sharpen our focus on the facets of academic careers and faculty roles that may be shifting and on differences among subgroups within the workforce. To illustrate, I have found (see Lawrence and others, 1990), as have other researchers (Trautvetter and Blackburn, 1990), that women in the sciences, when compared with their male peers, appear to be more likely to hold postdoctoral fellowships between graduate school and their first faculty appointment (a potential structural difference in the careers of males and females). A longitudinal study of appointment cohorts at a research university (Lawrence and Blackburn, 1985) showed that the number of publications at the time of initial employment rose dramatically between 1965 and 1970 (a normative change in careers). Various studies of faculty (see Blackburn and Lawrence, 1995, for a summary) reveal differences between times of data gathering in faculty evaluations and distribution of effort to teaching, research, and service activities (a normative shift in faculty roles). The data also show normative differences between subgroups of faculty (that is, humanities and science professors) at the different times of data gathering. And recent studies (for example, Gappa and Leslie, 1993) suggest that new faculty roles are emerging for part-time and adjunct faculty, where role-related tasks are typically restricted to teaching (structural changes in faculty roles).

The distinctions I am suggesting forewarn us about interchanging the characteristics of the workforce with characteristics of academic careers or faculty roles. They also underscore the importance of (1) recognizing variations among faculty from different types of institutions and from different academic areas and (2) distinguishing pervasive shifts in career norms and structures from temporary changes in the characteristics of individuals who entered the field or from changes in the workplace demands and resources at a particular time. Academic careers are situated in several contexts that affect their structures and norms—disciplines, geographic locations, institutions, gender, sociocultural, to name a few. Before we ask how careers are changing, it is reasonable to ask, What is *an academic career?*

Influences on Academic Careers

For the purpose of discussion, I have displayed selected practices in Table 2.1 and suggested how they might affect academic careers. These practices represent responses to diverse pressures from within and outside the academy: demographic characteristics of faculty and students, changes in the economy, funding for research, state and federal policies, and so forth. I have classified the practices in terms of their scope (effects on either or both academic career or faculty role) and in terms of their nature (structural or normative). The distinctions sharpen our perspective on academic careers and our capacity to assess the impact of part-time and adjunct faculty. I have taken the traditional tenure-track faculty appointment to be the modal academic career, and I focus in the following pages on administrative practices that may result in deviations from that pattern of ranks, activities, and responsibilities.

At least five general types of changes in the preparation and employment of faculty are discussed in the literature on academic careers—changes that (1) alter the normative aspects of academic careers and the faculty roles that make up an academic career, (2) affect only the normative aspect of careers, (3) affect career norms and structures as well as the normative aspects of faculty roles, (4) alter the normative aspects of faculty roles but do not change academic careers, and (5) result in structural and normative changes in careers and in faculty roles.

No Change in Career Structure. Subsumed here are practices that may alter career and role norms but not their basic structures. Ad hoc employment of part-time faculty typically does not change either the order of ranks a person occupies during an academic career or the time typically spent in each rank. However, this practice can influence the normative expectations regarding knowledge production among tenure-track professors. Institutional drift toward a single merit system has resulted in the "pursuit of prestige through faculty research productivity" (Fairweather, 1996, p. 204). The trend has been

Table 2.1. Effects of Higher Education Practices on Academic Career and Faculty Role

Higher Education Practices	Academic Career		Faculty Role	
	Structure[a]	Norms[b]	Structure[c]	Norms[d]
Employ part-time & full-time temporary faculty ad hoc		x	x	x
Alter emphases on teaching & scholarship in recruitment & hiring		x		x
Stop "tenure clock"		x		
Affirmative action	x	x		x
Delay entry to tenure-track positions	x	x		x
Reduced time to Ph.D.	x	x		x
Emeritus faculty as teachers	x	x		x
Entry reductions in teaching loads				x
Establish distinct appointment tracks: instructional & research	x	x	x	x
Alterations in tenure	x	x	x	x
Shared tenure-track positions	x	x	x	x
Recruit "stars"	x	x	x	x
Movement between administrative & faculty tracks	x	x	x	x
Third-year reviews	x	x	x	x
Virtual universities	x	x	x	x

Note: [a]Employment tracks, sequences of positions, access, and involvement; [b]felt pressure to choose particular tracks, attractiveness of tracks, ascribed legitimacy, performance criteria; [c]assigned activities and rights; [d]values and perceived pressures to behave in particular ways.

for colleges and universities to emulate the elite research universities and to hire faculty who will bring institutional recognition through their scholarship.

The opportunity to interact with esteemed scholars in and out of class is attractive to students, and institutions develop mechanisms to limit but not eliminate instructional contact with these "stars." The use of part-time or adjunct faculty to "supplement" tenure-track faculty by teaching courses while professors work on their research can heighten expectations for scholarship on campuses where the prior emphasis may have been more balanced or leaning toward teaching. On campuses where the emphasis has always been on research, the use of part-time faculty may have little discernible effect on career norms or faculty roles. I have not found written reports showing that the use of part-time or adjunct faculty permanently altered the structure of the faculty role by eliminating teaching responsibilities. In fact, some of the most prestigious research universities have policies restricting the number of courses from which a faculty member may be released.

On the one hand, ad hoc employment of part-time and adjunct faculty means that individuals who want to teach college students but do not want the pressure for research have career opportunities. However, part-time faculty free up tenure-track professors' time for research which, in turn, is likely to alter the normative expectations for role performance. Ironically, the part-time faculty may actually reduce their own chances of successfully competing for tenure-track appointments. Even if they are given credit for their time in rank, the gap in scholarship between themselves and those on the tenure track may continue to widen.

Recommendations to alter scholarly norms to accommodate research on teaching or to alter the criteria used to select faculty (see Boyer, 1990) are important and may influence the normative aspects of academic careers and faculty roles. However, this practice does not necessarily change the basic configuration of the faculty role; it still encompasses teaching, research, and service. Furthermore, for the kind of behavioral change Boyer and others envisioned (see Schön, 1995), a transformation in the unit of analysis in merit and reward decisions must take place as well. Blackburn and Lawrence (1995) and others have written that if such normative changes are to influence faculty values and behavior, the exclusive emphasis of individual contributions must be revised, the collective accomplishments of departments must be considered in merit decisions, and the standards for promotion and tenure must be reformed to reflect these changes.

Career Norms Only. I noted one practice that could alter career norms—stopping the "tenure clock" temporarily while a faculty member takes limited time for family care. Such practices do not, in and of themselves, lead to fundamental changes in academic careers or faculty roles. The norms still emphasize individual achievement and activity (Blackburn and Lawrence, 1995) and a faculty member only buys time to produce in traditional ways. However, the alteration does signal a value shift within the academy to temporarily accommodate non-work-related events in faculty work lives.

Career Structures and Norms and Faculty-Role-Related Norms. These are practices that alter careers but do not necessarily change the range of faculty-role-related activities. For example, postdoctoral fellowships delay entry to faculty positions in several fields, modify selection norms for hiring junior faculty by increasing scholarly expectations, and most likely affect the valuation of research among the newest cohort of assistant professors. However, this delayed entry does not necessarily mean that the structure of the faculty role is changed. The tenure-track faculty member still has responsibilities across the range of teaching, research, and service activities. The press in some disciplines to shorten the time in graduate school, combined with the push for sponsored research, has raised concern that scholarly norms—and ultimately what it means to be an intellectual—are affected. Educators are questioning whether people have time to read broadly and to reflect on the implications; they wonder what the long-term consequences of these normative changes are for the quality of faculty scholarship (Bean, 1997).

Affirmative action policies may have affected the normative aspect of academic careers by adjusting selection criteria. Some would argue that the impact of these policies is not only normative in the sense that the competition for faculty positions has been opened but the opportunity structure for majority group members has been altered. The literature (Johnsrud, 1993) and my current research (Lawrence and Patton, 1997) suggest that affirmative action practices may have some limited impact on role-related norms, such as the relative valuation of areas of expertise and avenues for the dissemination of scholarship. However, I see little evidence that the structural aspects of faculty roles are affected.

Faculty Role Norms Only. One practice in research universities is to give new tenure-track faculty members a chance to establish their programs of research by phasing them gradually into a full-time teaching load. This effort has affected the norms regarding how faculty should spend their time but has not altered the structure of the career or the faculty role in terms of its cluster of responsibilities. Within most academic areas, people still seem to move through the ranks at similar rates and in similar proportions, although institutions are often reluctant to share data that would illustrate attrition prior to the tenure decision. Thus the reporting of results regarding the proportion of faculty who gain tenure may be influenced.

Pervasive Changes. Some practices have profound effects on academic careers and faculty roles. Take, for example, the emerging "virtual universities," which could redefine academic careers altogether. Campuses may no longer exist as we know them today, and the terms *colleague* and *instruction* may have to be redefined. The implications of such organizational transformations are seemingly endless.

The elimination or revision of tenure policies is another practice that would likely have a major impact on academic careers. The differentiation of the career structure into ranks, for example, may become useless and disappear. The norms in terms of desirability of the faculty career among doctoral degree recipients in some fields may be altered. And the faculty role could shift dramatically as people are hired for a narrower range of activities and their commitment to the institution and investment in activities that enhance its prestige may shift away from a local orientation to one that ensures their own portability.

Some foreshadowing of the impact of tenure policy changes are evident in current practices. Consider, for example, contractual agreements that stipulate a formal review of junior tenure-track faculty and make reappointment contingent on the outcomes. Essentially, such agreements give the newly hired professor two or three years to initiate and establish programs of research and to become involved in the instructional activities of their departments. Probationary time is shortened, turnover typically increases, and institutional mobility may be altered. Faculty roles are affected structurally and normatively as department chairs try to nurture and "protect" assistant professors.

Shared appointments in which two faculty divide a single tenure-track position also challenge the structural and normative aspects of the academic career. Some questions that must be answered are: How is time in rank calculated? Do both people engage in research, teaching, and service, or are activities divided between them in some other way? What are the implications for performance evaluation and promotion?

The "trifurcation" of academic appointments into the traditional tenure track and distinct teaching and research tracks is another practice that can exert a pervasive influence. On some campuses, doctorally prepared teachers are hired in lecture and clinical teaching tracks where the focus is almost exclusively on instruction. Others hold appointments as research scientists and are expected to obtain and conduct sponsored research projects. These distinct academic career structures offer alternatives to tenure-track appointments, and each has different normative implications for an individual who might want to move to the tenure track.

Instructional demands in lower-division courses like English composition always outstrip the supply of tenure-track faculty to teach them. Sometimes the demand for faculty in an instructional area temporarily exceeds the supply; sometimes there is demand for specialized courses (for example, studio courses) or for instruction requiring highly specialized expertise (for example, in clinical practice courses). Ideal part-time faculty in these instances are able teachers who want to combine college teaching and nonacademic careers, who find teaching to be satisfying when combined with other work activities, or who find that part-time employment suits their lifestyle choices. An alternative career structure that combines college teaching with other professional activities outside academe may be taking shape. Along with it, many normative issues are rising with respect to these individuals' status within the institution, access to instructional services, and involvement in curricular and governance decisions.

When individuals desire full-time teaching and see a department's instructional needs as an opportunity for full-time teaching (an instructional career track), arrangements may be perceived as exploitative, depending on the institutional practices regarding benefits, resources, access to decision making, and so forth. Tenure-track faculty want to retain faculty who maintain consistency in the quality of undergraduate instruction and who reliably prepare students for upper-division courses. They also feel the pressure to enhance departmental stature through scholarship. This intersection between the lives of academics may well produce the most fundamental changes in careers, as people on different tracks negotiate with administrators for rights and responsibilities around such issues as resources and governance. Normative issues must be resolved (as noted earlier), along with more structural ones such as how to distinguish among non-tenure-track faculty who differ in years of service, level of instructional responsibility, and so forth.

Accommodating dual careers among faculty is a recruiting challenge for colleges and universities. When they fit with a candidate's lifestyle choices, part-time and adjunct faculty positions have been offered. However, such appointments may also be used to put people on hold, so to speak, allowing them initial entry into the institution until a tenure-track position opens up. For individuals in the latter situation, the arrangements can be career disappointments if key players do not act in good faith. Disruptions are probable in the lives of at least two faculty, not to mention the students with whom they work, and there is always a chance that the academy can lose faculty and students. An institution's accumulating practices in this area may alter career structures by developing formal mechanisms for moving across tracks and change the norms in terms of the range of responsibilities expected of adjunct faculty.

Colleges and universities are conservative organizations, especially when it comes to curricular change (Clark, 1987). Part-time faculty may serve a very useful purpose by meeting demonstrated needs for instruction in emerging areas. Career options for these individuals are affected by the extent to which a new area becomes central to the discipline or field. If it appears to be gaining recognition, adjuncts or part-time faculty could be moved to the tenure track to ensure continuity. However, they could be replaced with tenure-track faculty who decide to move into the new instructional and research area. The academic career structure and norms may be affected, depending on the mechanisms created to accommodate the pioneers (those who were there first) in an area and on how the area changes in terms of its stature in the eyes of faculty.

Finally, as colleges and universities recognize the importance of student-centered instruction, the need for teachers may increase. Student-centered teaching in such courses as music performance classes, supervised student teaching, and clinical courses in health-related fields is being introduced in more instructional areas and serves important purposes beyond the curricular, such as integrating first-year students into campus life. If such shifts to more labor-intensive instruction continue, demands for faculty will increase but they may also affect the selection of part-time faculty. Faculty expertise will have to extend beyond academic knowledge and encompass information about a particular campus. Should such changes occur, part-time faculty will need to assess their interest and capacity for teaching these courses, and postsecondary institutions will need to consider the structural and normative career implications regarding the use of part-time faculty. One would think it would become more difficult for the part-time faculty member to teach at multiple institutions and for the institution to hire such teachers without investing in their professional development.

Conclusion

How are academic careers changing? What are the implications for the character of the academy? The difficulty in projecting trends is that careers are situated in multiple contexts—disciplinary, institutional, and individual—and the available data provide snapshots at single points in time.

Intersections in the work lives of individuals on different career tracks and alterations in the preparation and employment of faculty, as well as the decisions and behavior of any one group within the academy, have demonstrable effects on others. To understand and assess how various factors affect academic careers, we must reach some agreement on the definitions that will guide our research and that will serve as a basis for our projections. Perhaps the framework presented in this chapter will move us along toward this goal.

References

Bean, J. P. "Alternative Models of Professorial Roles: New Languages to Reimagine Faculty Work." Paper presented at the annual meeting of the Association for the Study of Higher Education. Albuquerque, N.M., Nov. 1997.

Blackburn, R., and Lawrence, J. *Faculty at Work.* Baltimore: Johns Hopkins Press, 1995.

Boyer, E. *Scholarship Reconsidered: Priorities of the Professoriate.* Princeton, N.J.: Carnegie Foundation for the Advancement of Teaching, 1990.

Clark, B. *The Academic Life: Small Worlds, Different Worlds.* Princeton, N.J.: Carnegie Foundation for the Advancement of Teaching, 1987.

Fairweather, J. *Faculty Work and Public Trust.* Boston: Allyn & Bacon, 1996.

Finkelstein, M. J. *The American Academic Profession: A Synthesis of Social Scientific Inquiry since World War II.* Columbus: Ohio State University Press, 1984.

Gappa, J., and Leslie, D. *The Invisible Faculty.* San Francisco: Jossey-Bass, 1993.

Johnsrud, L. K. (ed.). *Women and Minority Faculty Experiences: Defining and Responding to Diverse Realities.* New Directions for Teaching and Learning no. 53. San Francisco: Jossey-Bass, 1993.

Lawrence, J., and Backburn, R. "Faculty Careers: Maturation, Demographic and Historical Effects." *Research in Higher Education,* 1985, 22 (2), 135–154.

Lawrence, J., and Patton, D. "Work Satisfaction and Faculty Departure among African American Faculty." Paper presented at the annual meeting of the Association for the Study of Higher Education, Albuquerque, N.M., Nov. 1997.

Lawrence, J., Blackburn, R., Trautvetter, L., Hart, K., and Herzberg, G. "Women in Selected 'Male' and 'Female' Disciplines: A View of Professional Behavior at Three Points in Time—1969, 1975, 1988." Paper presented at the annual meeting of the American Educational Research Association, Boston, Apr. 1990.

Schön, D. "The New Scholarship Requires a New Epistemology." *Change*. Nov./Dec. 1995, pp. 27–34.

Tierney, W. "Organizational Socialization in Higher Education." *Journal of Higher Education*, 1997, *68* (1), 1–16.

Trautvetter, L., and Blackburn, R. "Gender Differences in Predicting Faculty Publication Output in the Natural Sciences." Paper presented at the annual meeting of the American Educational Research Association, Boston, Apr. 1990.

JANET H. LAWRENCE is director of the Center for the Study of Higher and Postsecondary Education and associate professor, School of Education, University of Michigan, Ann Arbor.

Like adjunct faculty, professionals in nonstandard jobs frequently are paid lower wages, are less likely to receive health insurance or a pension from their employer, and have less job security than their counterparts in regular, full-time jobs.

The Changing Pattern of Employment Relations

M. Edith Rasell, Eileen Appelbaum

The use of nonstandard work arrangements appears to have increased slightly over the last two to three decades (see Table 3.1).Today, significant numbers of workers across the occupational spectrum are employed in nonstandard jobs. Nonstandard work is defined here as the absence of a regular, full-time, employer-employee relationship. Workers in nonstandard jobs include

- Independent contractors (freelancers or independent consultants)
- Contract workers (for example, computer specialists employed at a computer services firm that contracts to provide services to other firms, where the specialists spend their work time)
- On-call workers such as nurses and substitute teachers who are called in as needed
- Temps (workers employed by a temporary-help agency)
- Day laborers
- Self-employed people, such as business owners
- Workers employed in a regular employer-employee relationship who work less than thirty-five hours per week

Professional employees are about as likely as the general workforce to be employed as nonstandard workers (Spalter-Roth and others, 1997), whereas faculty members are far more likely than professional employees generally to be in such work arrangements (Gappa and Leslie, 1997).

Employment arrangements other than regular full-time jobs can make sense, provided they lead to new career paths or meet increased needs for flexibility on the part of both employers and workers. If, however, these arrangements are driven by employers' desire to reduce labor costs or if

Table 3.1. Employment in Nonstandard Arrangements
(Share of Nonagricultural Employment)

Year	Part-time			Temporary-Help Agency	Self-Employed
	Total	Involuntary	Voluntary		
1973	16.6%	3.1%	13.5%	n.a.	6.7%
1979	17.6	3.8	13.8	0.5%	7.1
1989	18.1	4.3	13.8	1.1	7.5
1993	18.8	5.5	13.3	1.5	7.7
1995	18.4	3.7	14.7	1.9	7.3
1996	18.1	3.5	14.6	2.0	7.1

Note: Part-time workers are a share of all persons at work. Data for part-time workers and the self-employed from the Bureau of Labor Statistics (BLS), Employment and Earnings Reports, various years. Temps are all people employed in the help supply services industry; data are from the BLS website, July 24, 1997; data prior to 1982 not available.

Source: Authors' analysis of February 1995 Current Population Survey data.

workers seeking regular full-time employment are forced to settle for nonstandard employment, such arrangements may fail to provide employees with the flexibility and economic security they require. Thus the quality of nonstandard jobs is the main concern, that is, whether they pay wages similar to those paid in regular full-time jobs to people with similar characteristics, are as likely as regular full-time jobs to provide fringe benefits, and provide an equivalent level of job security. Also of concern is whether such employment reflects the preferences of workers. The quality of nonstandard jobs is of heightened importance because the majority of nonstandard workers, including professionals generally and college faculty in particular, are women who may already be disadvantaged in the workplace in terms of wages and promotions.

The purpose of this chapter is to examine the quality of nonstandard work arrangements (NSWAs) and the preferences of workers for these jobs, focusing on nonstandard work arrangements among professionals. This analysis is drawn from a much larger study of nonstandard work arrangements among managers and professionals, based on a 1995 nationally representative survey of 58,000 workers, which we coauthored (Spalter-Roth and others, 1997). The experiences of college faculty in nonstandard employment were analyzed by Gappa and Leslie (1997), based on a 1993 survey of 7,000 nontenurable faculty, and are compared here to the experiences of professionals more generally. Our main conclusion is that the experiences of academics in nonstandard jobs are quite similar to those of other professionals in these arrangements in terms of job quality and worker preferences.

Defining Nonstandard Work Arrangements

An informed discussion of nonstandard work arrangements must begin with clear definitions. Nonstandard arrangements differ from standard jobs in at least one of the following ways:

- The absence of an employer, as in self-employment and independent contracting
- A distinction between the organization that employs the worker and the one for whom the person works, as in contract work and in working for temporary-help agencies
- The temporal instability of the job, as in temporary work, day labor, on-call work, and some forms of contracted work

In addition, nonstandard work arrangements include part-time employment in a standard employment relationship.

Researchers differ in the way they characterize nonstandard workers; nonstandard workers also categorize themselves in nonuniform ways. Gappa and Leslie (1997) conceptualize adjunct faculty as part-time employees and compare the characteristics and working conditions of these workers with those of full-time faculty. Yet many of these adjunct faculty members do not meet the criteria described earlier for regular, part-time employees. As Gappa and Leslie note, most adjuncts "are appointed term by term, and notification of an appointment or a renewal (regardless of the number of semesters previously employed) is often late" (p. 17). Their data show that 62 percent of so-called part-time faculty work on such term-by-term contracts (p. 12). Moreover, they note that these same workers often have heavy undergraduate teaching loads (p. 5).

In the February 1995 Current Population Survey, conducted by the U.S. Bureau of the Census for the Bureau of Labor Statistics (1997), respondents self-determined their type of work arrangement from the categories and examples given. Our analyses of these data use these self-defined categories of work arrangement to categorize workers.

We suspect that part-time faculty are paid like independent contractors, that is, they receive a 1099 form for income tax purposes, although they may not meet the legal definition for this classification. However, it is not clear that the CPS respondents identified themselves as independent contractors. In the CPS data, the modal detailed occupation for male professionals in standard part-time jobs is "postsecondary teacher," indicating that many adjunct faculty classify themselves as regular part-timers and not in a nonstandard relationship with an employer. Some probably appear in the data as independent contractors, whereas others may even classify themselves as on-call[1] or as other types of nonstandard workers. Here we are focusing on data for nonstandard professionals as a whole, as well as for those categorized as independent contractors and regular part-time workers. In most respects, the results for each of these groups of workers are similar. They differ, however, in the reasons workers are in nonstandard jobs and in workers' preferences for regular full-time employment. Adjunct faculty are most similar to on-call workers in this regard.

Trends Over Time

The proportion of full-time, tenured, or tenure-track faculty teaching undergraduate courses in community colleges, liberal arts colleges, and universities has declined dramatically since 1970. Data assembled from several sources by Gappa and Leslie (1997, p. 4) show that the share of regular full-time faculty employed in colleges and universities fell from 78 percent of total faculty employment in 1970–71 to 68 percent in 1982–83 and to 59 percent a decade later. This growth in nonstandard work arrangements for a largely white (89 percent) and highly educated (52 percent have a master's degree; 26 percent have a doctorate or terminal professional degree) workforce (pp. 9–10) appears to have outpaced the overall increase in such work arrangements in the United States. By 1993, 41 percent of faculty were in nonstandard jobs, and college teachers in nonstandard work arrangements were more likely than full-time faculty to be women—45 percent women and 33 percent men (p. 9).

Data on the overall growth of nonstandard work arrangements are currently not available. However, by 1995 fully 29.4 percent of workers (some 37 million people) were in nonstandard jobs: 34.4 percent of female workers and 25.4 percent of males. Tables 3.2 and 3.3 show the distribution of nonstandard work in the population. The first nationally representative survey that queried respondents about all the types of nonstandard work in which they might have been engaged was the February 1995 supplement to the CPS. The survey was repeated in February of 1998, which means researchers will be able to trace the changes in nonstandard work since 1995. There are no data for years before that time.

Other labor market surveys, however, can be used to examine the growth in three types of nonstandard work: part-time work, temporary (agency) workers, and the self-employed. (Although the data from these surveys are consistent across years, because of variations in the questions asked, they are not consistent with data from the February 1995 survey.) Data from the monthly CPS show that part-time workers as a share of all people at work in nonagricultural employment rose 1.5 percentage points between 1973 and 1996, from 16.6 percent to 18.1 percent (Mishel, Bernstein, and Schmitt, 1997; U.S. Department of Labor, 1997).[2] The rate rose from 18.1 percent in 1989 to 18.8 percent in 1993, but as the economic expansion continued, the rate in 1996 returned to its 1989 level. Involuntary part-time employment, which generally declines during periods of low unemployment, has fallen from its 1989 level of 5.5 percent, or 29 percent of all part-timers. In 1996 involuntary part-time workers were 3.5 percent of employment and 19 percent of all part-timers. The most rapid growth in NSWAs occurred in temporary-help agency employment, which rose from 0.5 percent of all nonagricultural employment in 1982 to 2.0 percent in 1996. Self-employment, including both sole proprietors and inde-

Table 3.2. Workers by Work Arrangement

Work Arrangement	Total	Women	Men	White	Black	Hispanic	Other
Regular part-time	13.7%	21.3%	7.1%	13.7%	13.2%	13.8%	14.1%
Temporary-help agency	1.0	1.1	0.8	0.8	1.9	1.3	1.0
On call/Day labor	1.6	1.7	1.5	1.5	1.7	2.5	1.7
Self-employment	5.5	4.8	6.1	6.3	1.5	3.2	5.5
Independent contracting-WS[a]	0.9	0.9	0.9	0.9	0.7	0.8	1.0
Independent contracting-SE[b]	5.6	3.7	7.3	6.4	2.4	3.3	4.2
Contract company	1.2	0.8	1.6	1.2	1.1	1.3	1.7
All nonstandard	29.4	34.4	25.4	30.8	22.4	26.2	29.2
Regular full-time	70.6	65.7	74.7	69.2	77.6	73.7	70.9
Total	100%	100.0%	100.0%	100.0%	100.0%	100.0%	100.0%

[a]Wage and salary; [b]self-employment.

Source: Adapted from Kalleberg and others, 1997, p. 9.

Table 3.3. Occupational Group by Work Arrangement (%)

Work Arrangement	Managerial	Professional	Other White Collar[a]	Blue Collar[b]
Regular part-time	4.4%	12.3%	18.4%	13.9%
Temporary-help agency	0.5	0.5	1.1	1.2
On call/Day labor	0.3	2.2	0.8	2.3
Self-employment	9.4	4.2	5.3	4.8
Independent contracting-WS[c]	0.6	1.2	1.0	0.8
Independent contracting-SE[d]	8.2	5.8	3.9	6.0
Contract company	0.8	1.8	0.7	1.4
All nonstandard	24.2	28.0	31.2	30.4
Regular full-time	75.7	71.9	68.7	69.6
Total	100%	100.0%	100.0%	100.0%

[a]Technicians, sales, and administrative support occupations; [b]private household, protective service, and other service occupations; craft and transportation occupations; machine operators; laborers; farming; forestry; and fishery occupations; [c]wage and salary; [d]self-employment.

Source: Spalter-Roth, Kalleberg, Rasell, and others, 1997, p. 5.

pendent contractors, rose from 6.7 percent in 1973 to 7.1 percent in 1996. Although there are no longitudinal data on other types of nonstandard work, most observers believe there has been a large growth in these types of employment arrangements as well. However, the growth of part-time faculty likely exceeds the growth in NSWAs as a whole.

Job Quality

We compare standard (regular, full-time) and nonstandard jobs on three dimensions: wages, receipt of health insurance or a pension from a worker's own employer, and job security. We begin by summarizing Gappa and Leslie's (1997) findings. We then report our own findings for professional workers from the analysis of the February 1995 data.

Faculty employed in NSWAs earn far less than full-time faculty in tenured or tenure-track positions. Gappa and Leslie (1997) suggest that, adjusting for instruction time, a full-time faculty member typically receives $4,000 per course compared to $1,500 for the part-time college teacher (p. 15). They find that very few institutions provide benefits for part-timers. Only 17 percent receive employer-sponsored health insurance for which the employer pays at least some of the costs, compared with 97 percent of full-timers; only 20 percent had an employer who contributed to their pension, compared with 93 percent of full-time faculty (p. 18). And they note that adjunct faculty have no job security. Some of these faculty members have had stable employment histories, but this is the result of institutional good will and not of any right to job security (p. 19). Similar results can be noted for professional workers in NSWAs generally; they earn lower wages, have far fewer benefits, and less job security than their counterparts in regular, full-time employment.

Wages. Holding constant some demographic characteristics including education, we find that regular, part-time male and female professionals earn 24 and 10 percent less per hour, respectively, than regular full-time professionals. Male professionals working as independent contractors face a pay penalty of 13 percent; among women, the pay difference is not statistically significant. The pay penalties for male and female on-call workers are 30 and 21 percent, respectively; women who are self-employed have a pay penalty of 19 percent.

Among nonstandard workers of all occupations, we have identified wage penalties similar to those presented here for professionals. Moreover, when we examine nonstandard workers by education level, we find the differentials persist even with higher levels of schooling. In most types of nonstandard work, the pay penalty for a nonstandard worker with a high school diploma compared to a regular full-time worker with this level of education is little different, on average, than that for college-educated standard and nonstandard workers. For example, women *temps* with a high school diploma face a penalty that averages 19 percent, whereas with a college degree the penalty averages 21 percent. For male *temps*, the penalties are 25 and 21 percent, respectively, for those with a high school and college education. Although many policymakers argue that higher education is the key to a rising standard of living, additional schooling does not appear to allow nonstandard workers to overcome the pay differentials.

Employer-Sponsored Health Insurance and Pensions. Professionals in NSWAs receive health insurance or a pension from their employer much less often than regular full-time workers in these occupations. Just 48.1 percent of female and 49.0 percent of male professionals working in regular part-time jobs receive either of these benefits. For on-call workers the percentages are 30.6 and 43.0 percent, respectively (see Table 3.4). (All self-employed independent contractors must purchase their own health insurance and pension.) In general, professionals in nonstandard jobs receive these benefits at less than half the rate of regular full-time professionals.

Job Security. Another important dimension of job quality is job security—whether with a satisfactory performance, a worker may continue in a job indefinitely. We define a job to be of uncertain duration if a respondent (1) reports his job is temporary, (2) reports he cannot work for his employer as long as he wishes, (3) is not sure about criteria 1 or 2, or (4) expects his job to last for one year or less. Nonstandard workers face relatively high rates of job insecurity. Among regular full-time professionals, just 6.4 percent of women and 7.5 percent of men work in jobs of uncertain duration. But among professionals in nonstandard work, fully 25.4 percent of women and 20.9 percent of men are in insecure jobs. (See Table 3.5.) Among part-time faculty, job insecurity rates are likely even higher, given the practice of term-by-term appointments.

Preferences for Nonstandard Work

Most workers in nonstandard jobs prefer this type of work arrangement. This is true of adjunct faculty as well; more than half (52 percent) indicate that they prefer part-time work, whereas 43 percent report that they could not find a full-time position in their field (Gappa and Leslie, 1997, p. 11). These are higher rates of preference for full-time, presumably standard work than is true for professional nonstandard workers as a whole.

In the CPS data, 11.3 percent of female professionals and 12.3 percent of men were working in regular part-time jobs because they could not find full-time work. (See Table 3.6.) Among on-call professionals, the rates were even higher: 42.7 and 48.6 percent for women and men, respectively. Another way of examining this question is to observe the share of professionals in NSWA who would prefer a regular full-time job. We note that 20.1 percent of women professionals and 15.5 percent of men report that they prefer but cannot find regular full-time employment. (See Table 3.7.) Among regular, part-time professionals, 16.6 percent of women and 22.0 percent of men prefer full-time work—much lower rates than for part-time faculty. Adjunct faculty are markedly more dissatisfied with their work arrangements than are professional nonstandard workers as a whole.

Table 3.4. Professionals with Health Insurance or Pension by Work Arrangement and Sex

Work Arrangement	Women	Men
Regular part-time	48.1%	49.0%
Temporary-help agency	40.4	5.0
On-call	30.6	43.0
Independent contracting-WS[a]	19.5	41.1
Contract company	74.8	73.4
Regular full-time	92.2	93.8

[a]Wage and salary.

Source: Spalter-Roth, Kalleberg, Rasell, and others, 1997, p. 48.

Table 3.5. Jobs of Uncertain Duration by Work Arrangement and Sex

Work Arrangement	Female Professional	Male Professional
Regular part-time	16.3%	31.5%
Temporary-help agency	54.6	84.0
On call/Day labor	100.0	100.0
Self-employment	5.3	4.5
Independent contracting-WS[a]	50.0	36.9
Independent contracting-SE[b]	10.3	8.0
Contract company	17.0	24.1
All nonstandard	25.4%	20.9%
Regular full-time	6.4	7.5
All	12.3%	10.8%

[a]Wage and salary; [b]self-employment

Source: Spalter-Roth, Kalleberg, Rasell, and others, 1997, p. 53.

Table 3.6. Professionals Who Work in NSWAs Because They Cannot Find Other Employment, by Nonstandard Work Arrangement and Sex

Work Arrangement	Women	Men
Regular part-time	11.3%	12.3%
Temporary-help agency	50.0	76.5
On call	42.7	48.6
Self-employment	2.1	1.3
Independent contracting	7.9	6.0
Total	15.0	9.4

Source: Spalter-Roth, Kalleberg, Rasell, and others, 1997, p. 29.

Table 3.7. Professionals Who Would Prefer a Regular Job, by Nonstandard Work Arrangement, and Sex

Work Arrangement	Women	Men
Regular part-time	16.6%	22.0%
Temporary-help agency	35.3	92.3
On call	56.6	60.0
Self-employment	6.7	5.6
Independent contracting	12.1	11.6
Total	20.1	15.5

Source: Spalter-Roth, Kalleberg, Rasell, and others, 1997, p. 29.

Conclusion

Nonstandard work is, on average, of lower quality than regular full-time employment. Workers are paid less, receive health insurance or pensions less often, and enjoy less job security than their counterparts in regular full-time employment. Surprisingly, this is as true of professional employees in NSWAs as it is of less well-educated workers. It is also true of adjunct faculty. These sharp differentials in wages, benefits, and job security provide many employers with perverse incentives to make excessive use of nonstandard work arrangements. In the case of departments and institutions that employ adjunct faculty, Gappa and Leslie (1997) found that employing faculty on this basis as a money-saving tactic "leads to using part-timers for the wrong reasons" (p. 15), with adverse effects on the effectiveness of these teachers and on their contributions to academic quality. Moreover, they note that wages are only part of the labor cost associated with employing college teachers. Other costs include hiring, orientation, supervision, evaluation, space, equipment, and support services, all of which may be higher for adjunct than for regular faculty.

The effect of being in a NSWA on the lives of individuals is somewhat more difficult to evaluate for professionals. Household income for these individuals is likely to place them in the middle of the family income distribution or higher. In the case of adjunct faculty, 77 percent have jobs elsewhere, and fewer than 11 percent have annual household incomes under $25,000 (Gappa and Leslie, 1997, p. 11). This is hardly surprising because adjunct jobs typically pay $1,500 per course, and even a full course load of three or four courses a semester would only pay between $9,000 and $12,000 a year. For those who hold adjunct positions because they want to be part of an academic environment (71 percent, according to Gappa and Leslie, 1997, p. 11), teaching one or two courses a semester while working elsewhere may eliminate financial hardship, but the cost in terms of dashed ambitions may nevertheless be high. Gappa and Leslie's proposal for reforming the employment relationship for adjunct faculty by "reconceptualizing the [college] workforce as one faculty that shares work equitably, that collaborates on designing and conducting high-quality experiences for students, that concentrates on setting high standards for all" (p. 8) would go a long way toward providing these workers with the opportunities and incentives to do their jobs well while improving academic quality for students. If we add that the rewards for work should also be shared equitably, then this is a formula for ending the "duality" of nonstandard versus standard employment relations that could be applied widely to workers in NSWAs.

Notes

1. Respondents who report that they work on-call were wage and salary workers who answered yes to the following question: "Some people are in a pool of workers who are *only* called to work as needed, although they can be scheduled to work for several days or weeks in a row, for example, substitute teachers and construction workers supplied by a union hiring hall. These people are sometimes referred to as 'on-call' workers. Were you an on-call worker last week?"

2. These figures differ from those we report from the February 1995 supplement because they include all workers, both standard and nonstandard, with fewer than thirty-five hours of work per week. In the analysis of the February 1995 data, we first categorize workers by their primary employee-employer relationship and only secondarily by the number of hours worked. Thus, a temp working twenty hours a week would be classified as a temp, not a part-time worker; all part-time workers have regular employee-employer relationships.

References

Gappa, J. M., and Leslie, D. W. "Two Faculties or One?: The Conundrum of Part-Timers in a Bifurcated Work Force." American Association for Higher Education, Inquiry no.6, 1997.

Kalleberg, A. L., Rasell, E., Cassirer, N., Reskin, B. F., Hudson, K., Webster, D., Appelbaum, E., and Spalter-Roth, R. M. *Nonstandard Work, Substandard Jobs: Flexible Work Arrangements in the U.S.* Washington, D.C.: Economic Policy Institute, 1997.

Mishel, L., Bernstein, J., and Schmitt, J. *The State of Working America, 1996–1997.* Economic Policy Institute Series. Armonk, N.Y.: M. E. Sharpe, 1997.

Spalter-Roth, R. M., Kalleberg, A. L., Rasell, E., Cassirer, N., Reskin, B. F., Hudson, K., Webster, D., Appelbaum, E., and Dooley, B. L. *Managing Work and Family: Nonstandard Work Arrangements Among Managers and Professionals.* Washington, D.C.: Economic Policy Institute and Women's Research and Education Institute, 1997.

U.S. Department of Labor, Bureau of Labor Statistics. *Employment and Earnings* (January). Washington, D.C.: U.S. Government Printing Office, 1997.

M. EDITH RASELL *is a labor and health economist at the Economic Policy Institute in Washington, D.C.*

EILEEN APPELBAUM *is associate research director at the Economic Policy Institute in Washington, D.C.*

The distribution of teaching, research, and service among different categories of "subfaculty" results in benefits of division of labor but also harmful effects of status differential.

The Subfaculty

Donald N. Langenberg

The questions addressed in this chapter are, Why do research universities employ postdoctoral fellows, graduate teaching assistants, adjuncts, and part-timers? What determines the mix? I shall try to answer these questions first. Then I will take advantage of this platform to make some observations about what I believe this discussion is really about.

Graduate Teaching Assistants

Research universities employ graduate teaching assistants for two reasons. One is that they provide a means to support regular faculty in their teaching functions by delegating responsibility for some of the more routine and arduous aspects of teaching, especially in large classes, thus permitting the regular faculty to focus on the creative intellectual management of the student learning process. This could of course be done by appropriately qualified staff persons, perhaps at comparable overall cost. But research universities by definition have substantial numbers of graduate students. These students are selected for their academic qualifications; they are generally thought to have the potential to join the next generation of faculty scholars; and they need the money. It makes good sense, therefore, to employ graduate students as teaching assistants. From the students' perspective, it helps solve the problem of keeping body and soul together on the way to a doctorate, and it provides useful practical experience in doing what some (but by no means all) will do for a living in the future. From the institution's perspective, the marginal cost of providing this support and experience (in the form of stipends and tuition waivers) is probably lower than it would be using regular staff, given the fact that the graduate students would be there anyway.

Graduate Research Assistants

Research universities also employ graduate research assistants who conduct research, sometimes simply as support staff to faculty engaged in their own scholarly work but more often in satisfaction of the dissertation requirement for the degree they are pursuing. The latter is most common in disciplines such as the sciences in which substantial external grant or contract support is available. Graduate research stipends are usually provided by the grant or contract. The mutual benefits are obvious. The graduate student gets paid to do what must be done anyway to earn a degree. The faculty supervisor gets quality help in achieving larger research objectives. And the institution is aided in preparing the next generation of researchers. Occasionally, a graduate student's work will result in the award of a Nobel Prize (sometimes to the student), and everybody can then bask in its glow.

Postdoctoral Fellows

Although they are technically employed by universities or other research institutions, so-called postdocs are generally employed by individual faculty researchers. For the fellow, such employment provides an opportunity to make the transition from supervised apprentice researcher to full-fledged independent researcher under the tutelage of a leader in the field through one or more (sometimes many more) years of intensive full-time research work. For the employing researcher, it is a way of adding substantial intellectual horsepower to his or her research program at a relatively modest cost, typically something between that of a graduate student and a junior faculty colleague. This system really works. A study of Nobel laureates has suggested that the best way to enhance one's chances of winning a Nobel Prize is to have a Nobel laureate as a biological parent or, failing that, by doing a postdoc with one.

Of all the categories of research university employment considered here, that of postdoctoral fellow is generally the least well defined and regulated.

I would include in this category the interns or residents in medicine and some other health professions. Their experience is also designed to move them from closely supervised apprentices to relatively independent practitioners. They are the workhorses of every teaching hospital and, like postdocs, can fairly be described as overworked and underpaid.

Adjunct Faculty

I understand the term *adjunct faculty* generally to mean persons whose primary professional employment lies outside the university. Their adjunct faculty appointments within the university permit them to contribute their knowledge and skills to enhancing its academic programs and the work of its regular faculty in the canonical functions of teaching, research, and professional service. The term encompasses a diverse array of circumstances. For example, all of the following might be adjunct faculty: a writer or a string quartet in residence, a business executive who teaches a course in a business school on the management of telecommunications systems, a lawyer who teaches a course in a law school on telecommunications law, a federal laboratory researcher who supervises the dissertation research of a physics graduate student, a surgeon who supervises medical students on rotation in her hospital department. Adjunct faculty are generally employed because they can supplement, complement, and enrich the opportunities a university can offer its students through its regular faculty. The cost of adjunct faculty is not usually of great concern either to the university or to the individual. Adjuncts usually teach or participate otherwise in the life of the university because they find it personally rewarding and simply enjoy it. Their monetary compensation is typically minimal and sometimes nothing.

Part-Time Faculty

The term *part-time faculty* literally should mean persons who are employed by a university to perform some typical faculty function (that is, teaching, research, or professional service) but who do not or cannot commit their full and complete professional efforts to the purposes of the university in a manner typical of regular faculty. But that technically correct definition is not entirely satisfactory. Its category does not overlap the previously mentioned categories, all of which (except the postdoctoral fellows category) comprise part-timers, by definition. Further, it is susceptible to ambiguity resulting from uncertainty in the meaning of the term *full time*. Does that mean a standard forty-hour week? Or are we talking about the average faculty work week of fifty to sixty hours, or the eighty-hour week common among many other professionals, not to mention mothers of small children? And what about the person who has a part-time faculty position and works at it fifty hours a week?

Be that as it may, having acknowledged the deficiencies of the *part-time* label, we are probably stuck with it. For present purposes, I will define *part-time faculty* as persons employed by a university, usually to teach, in positions that carry few if any of the elements of compensation, benefits, or status enjoyed by regular faculty members. Such persons are employed because they enable the university to respond to short-term fluctuations in student demand or to persistent student demand in circumstances of severe financial stringency. Their academic qualifications are often comparable with those of regular faculty, though they may have been unable to find employment in a regular faculty position or their ability to handle a full-time job may be compromised by other important obligations, like child rearing. (The latter circumstance doubtless contributes to the observed disproportion of women among part-time faculty.) The cost of part-time faculty is a major concern to both the university and the part-time faculty—to the former because the part-time faculty market allows the university to get good work done cheaply and to the latter because that market sets compensation levels for part-time faculty well below those of their regular faculty counterparts.

That is my answer to the question, Why do research universities employ postdoctoral fellows, graduate teaching assistants, adjuncts, and part-timers? As to the question, What determines the mix?, I would say the mix is determined largely by institutional mission. It is not a matter of managerial choice because the occupants of the categories as I have defined them are not really interchangeable. The most evident possible area of fungibility is teaching that might be done either by graduate teaching assistants or by part-time faculty. But even there, a research university will tend to meet its need with graduate teaching assistants because it has lots of them, while a master's-level or comprehensive university will use part-time faculty because it doesn't have doctoral students.

Problems Related to Part-Time Faculty Employment.

The title and agenda of the Sloan Conference to which this chapter was originally addressed suggest that the roles of the categories of university employees have somehow become an issue requiring attention. Anyone who has not spent the last decade living in an outlying suburb of Ulan Bator might have reached the same conclusion by listening to faculty members, legislators, alumni, parents, businesspersons, or talk-show commentators, or by following popular press pundits. So what's the problem?

It is clear that there is considerable concern and unease among the informed public. Following is a sampler of assertions I have heard or read, listed roughly in the order of employment categories used earlier.

My daughter's being taught by graduate students instead of real professors. I'm outraged! That's not what I'm paying tuition for.

It's a pity we can't get faculty to teach freshmen. They'd do a lot better job than the TAs, of course.

TAs are slave labor. The only way they'll ever get decent treatment is to unionize, just like the clerical staff.

There's nothing hard about teaching. Anybody who wants to be a professor some day should be a TA in my course, listen to all my lectures, and just do what I do.

You can tell the quality of a faculty member by how many research assistants he has. Big grants and a big research group with lot's of RAs—that's the name of the game.

A postdoc is just a warehouse in which to stash a new Ph.D. until he or she can get a faculty position. They ought to give us humanists some of those instead of giving them all to the fat-cat scientists.

The sole purpose of real Ph.D. programs is to train future faculty members. The difficulty our Ph.D.'s have in finding good faculty jobs shows there are too many second-rate Ph.D. programs out there. Somebody ought to close them down.

A full-time tenured faculty is the only guarantee of quality.

Tenure is the problem. Get rid of that and you'll get rid of most of your other problems.

Shared governance is a cardinal academic value, one essential to the existence of a vital collegial academic community. No one who is not a tenured or tenure-track faculty member should be allowed to participate in shared governance.

Curricular matters are the province of the committed regular faculty. No adjunct or part-time faculty member could have anything significant to contribute to curriculum or academic program design.

Quality schmality! The only reason the tenured faculty are worried about part-time faculty is they're afraid we'll find out we can do just as well without them.

This sampler of concerns is ample indication of serious questions. Yet I am left with the uneasy feeling that there is really not much factual basis for concluding that there is some underlying problem here (or perhaps several), that we know what it is, and that we know what needs to be done to solve it. There is no doubt, for example, that the proportion of part-time faculty in many institutions has been growing, for fairly evident reasons. But where is the evidence that this has been demonstrably bad for students? I am prepared to engage in vigorous academic argument against each of the assertions in my sampler, in some cases with facts, or at least anecdotal evidence. But at the same time, I believe it would be irresponsible to tie my institutions' futures to a particular position on any of them, pro or con, based on what I believe is really known about them. If we could succeed in identifying one or two well-framed questions for serious further investigation, I think we would be making progress.

I am certain of one thing, however, based on nearly fifty years of experience in many different roles in higher education. If one considers the very different categories I have described and asks what the individuals in them have in common, the answer is not much—except for one thing. They are all defined by what they are not: they are not "regular" faculty. That would simply be a fact of life, not a problem, were it not for the propensity of our status-conscious regular faculty, and hence our institutions, to think of them and to treat them as if they were lesser species. Thus they are not just "nonfaculty," or "irregular faculty," they are "subfaculty." That is the point of the title I have chosen. We have all seen, in other sectors of our society, what damage such an attitude can cause. If there is an underlying problem here, I think that is it.

It seems to me that if we could only learn to recognize the members of our subfaculty as true partners in the grand calling of teaching and learning—partners with different but equally important roles—and enlist them as regular members of our collegium in all its functions, then we would ameliorate if not solve all the other problems before us. Let us eradicate the word *status* from our vocabularies and our behavior. At a time when the work of the academy and its members is changing more rapidly and radically than at any time in living memory, that may be the key to our continued success—and perhaps survival.

DONALD N. LANGENBERG is chancellor of the University System of Maryland.

Data from the 1993 National Study of Postsecondary Faculty show that part-time faculty are diverse.

Variations in the Characteristics of Part-Time Faculty by General Fields of Instruction and Research

Ernst Benjamin

The aggregate data on part-time faculty do not reveal the great diversity among these faculty. This chapter draws on data from the 1993 National Study of Postsecondary Faculty to explore certain differences among those part-time faculty who teach credit classes and designate teaching as their principal responsibility. It focuses especially on differences based on part-time faculty members' designated "principal teaching or research field." After a preliminary comparison of the twenty-six general fields into which the study grouped some 150 disciplines, I identify two clusters that differ substantially; each is composed of eight general fields: a *vocationally oriented cluster* (VOC) and a *liberal-arts-oriented cluster* (LAC). The VOC cluster includes first-professional health, nursing, occupational programs, law, business, engineering, physical sciences, and teacher education. The LAC cluster includes eight liberal arts fields: history, English and literature, foreign languages, fine arts, sociology, philosophy and religion, biological sciences, and political sciences.

The differences between these clusters suggest research directions that may better explain apparent contradictions in assessments of the quality, attitudes, and contributions of part-time faculty.

Distribution of Part-Time Faculty Among Disciplines

Part-time faculty are widely dispersed among the various disciplines. Table 5.1 displays this variation across the twenty-six general "teaching or research

All of the data used in this chapter are derived from the data collected in Fall 1992 by the National Study of Postsecondary Faculty (NSOPF), which was made available on the "Public Access Data Analysis System" CD-ROM prepared by the National Center for Education Statistics of the U.S. Department of Education.

Table 5.1. Proportion of Faculty Full- and Part-Time by Teaching or Research Field

| | All Faculty by Field | Appointment and Employment Status | | | | | |
| | | Two-Year Faculty | | Four-Year Faculty | | All Faculty | |
		Full-Time	Part-Time	Full-Time	Part-Time	Full-Time	Part-Time
English and literature	8.2%	38.3%	61.7%	55.4%	44.6%	47.1%	52.9%
Business	7.7	36.8	63.2	58.3	41.7	49.5	50.5
Fine arts	6.8	27.0	73.0	54.4	45.6	47.1	52.9
First-professional health	6.9	25.1	74.8	55.7	44.3	52.7	47.3
Math and statistics	5.4	30.1	69.9	70.1	29.9	47.8	52.2
All other programs	5.7	36.0	64.0	61.2	38.8	53.0	47.0
Other education	4.9	39.3	60.7	57.0	43.0	52.0	48.0
Other health science	4.0	41.3	58.7	53.3	46.7	48.2	51.8
Psychology	3.6	30.4	69.6	55.4	44.6	46.8	53.2
Occupation programs	3.6	41.7	58.3	62.6	37.4	47.2	52.8
Biological sciences	5.4	43.6	56.4	78.8	21.2	66.1	33.9
Computer sciences	2.9	31.3	68.7	61.5	38.5	45.3	54.7
Law	2.3	9.3	90.7	42.0	58.0	34.8	65.3
Teacher education	2.8	28.9	71.1	53.6	46.4	48.4	51.6
Engineering	3.8	43.3	56.7	73.0	27.0	63.7	36.3
Physical sciences	4.2	46.3	53.7	76.5	23.5	67.8	32.2
Foreign languages	2.6	24.9	75.1	62.9	37.1	52.5	47.5
Communications	2.1	30.7	69.3	49.3	50.7	45.0	55.0
Nursing	3.3	69.8	30.2	71.8	28.2	70.9	29.1
Other social science	2.0	37.2	62.8	62.2	37.8	56.0	44.0
History	2.3	45.0	55.0	70.9	29.1	62.6	37.4
Sociology	1.5	45.0	55.0	69.4	30.6	62.8	37.2
Agriculture/home economics	2.0	56.5	43.5	79.6	20.4	72.9	27.1
Philosophy and religion	1.3	23.5	76.5	72.9	27.1	63.2	36.8
Economics	1.3	46.2	53.8	79.9	20.1	72.6	27.4
Political sciences	1.2	55.4	44.6	77.8	22.2	72.7	27.3
Total	100.0	37.6	62.4	61.9	38.1	53.0	47.0

Note: In this and the tables that follow, the sample includes all faculty engaged in credit instruction who designated teaching as their principal activity.

fields." The fields are ranked by their proportion of all part-time faculty; the percentage of all faculty is multiplied by the percentage of part-time faculty.

Note that the fields contributing the highest numbers of part-time faculty include both vocational (business, health) and liberal arts (English, fine arts, mathematics) fields. Fields contributing relatively few part-time faculty are primarily liberal-arts-oriented except for agriculture and home economics. Some fields with relatively high percentages of part-time faculty, such as law and communications, are only in the mid-range of Table 5.1 because these fields have relatively fewer faculty altogether. Although the use of part-time faculty varies widely among fields, neither the ranking based on the proportion of all part-time faculty nor the ranking by the part-time percentage manifests a systematic variation based on the vocational and liberal arts clusters.

The reliance on part-time faculty in fields such as business, health, and law is in accord with the common argument that part-time faculty often bring their workplace skills to the university. Reliance on part-time faculty in English and math, however, is consistent with the argument that part-time faculty are heavily employed in core academic subjects. The two fields that contribute the most to part-time employment—English and business—are similar in that the percentage of part-time faculty in each of these fields is well above the percentage overall; that is, their disproportionate contribution to part-time employment is not simply a reflection of their larger contribution to faculty employment in general. Note, however, that in two-year colleges, business relies more than English on part-time faculty and that in four-year colleges, English is more reliant. Basically, the variations in reliance on part-time faculty across fields appear to reflect, but do not resolve, the contending perspectives that part-time faculty (1) bring outside skills and (2) replace full-time teachers in core academic subjects.

Two- and four-year institutions vary notably in their proportionate reliance on part-time faculty in some liberal arts disciplines. The relative reliance on part-time faculty in two-year colleges compared to four-year institutions is substantially higher for philosophy and religion, foreign languages, and math and statistics. English, as noted earlier, and communications are relatively more reliant on part-time faculty in four-year schools. The latter probably signals the greater reliance on part-time faculty to teach small, lower-division sections in four-year schools. The former may reflect the availability of part-time faculty relative to full-time faculty for religion and languages in two-year schools. The variance in mathematics may reflect the fact that two-year schools offer more remedial math than four-year schools. Or it may reflect a greater reliance on the format common in four-year schools: large lecture sections and small, graduate-student-led discussion groups. In any case, it is clear that some variations in disciplinary reliance on part-time faculty reflect their specific curriculum and pedagogy rather than interdisciplinary tendencies.

Qualifications of Part-Time Faculty

The most common measure of faculty professional preparation is the Ph.D. or professional degree. As Table 5.2 shows, part-time faculty, even controlling for

Table 5.2. Proportion of Full- and Part-Time Faculty with Ph.D. or Professional Degrees By Principal Teaching or Research Field

| | Faculty with Ph.D. and/or Professional Degrees | | | | | |
| | Part-Time | | Full-Time | | Four-Year Part-Time/Four-Year Full-Time | Two-Year Part-Time/Two-Year Full-Time |
	Four-Year	Two-Year	Four-Year	Two-Year		
Law	99.0%	79.8%	99.1%	n.d.	1.0%	
First-professional health	94.0	n.d.	93.8	n.d.	1.0	
Sociology	57.2	45.1	89.0	26.5	0.6	1.7
Psychology	54.2	21.8	92.8	45.1	0.6	0.5
Philosophy and religion	53.7	28.9	87.5	n.d.	0.6	
Biological sciences	51.4	33.0	93.4	29.5	0.6	1.1
Physical sciences	48.1	19.2	91.2	43.5	0.5	0.4
History	47.3	24.3	88.0	38.1	0.5	0.6
Political sciences	45.3	n.d.	93.2	34.0	0.5	
Other health science	44.1	9.1	62.4	7.2	0.7	1.3
Other education	41.7	10.4	83.0	16.7	0.5	0.6
Engineering	40.5	8.3	83.7	10.5	0.5	0.8
Other social science	39.3	26.7	80.2	33.9	0.5	0.8
All other programs	28.9	9.0	66.4	6.4	0.4	1.4
Mathematics and statistics	25.0	10.2	74.6	20.4	0.3	0.5
Business	23.2	10.1	68.2	15.6	0.3	0.6
Foreign languages	22.8	14.4	76.6	39.3	0.3	0.4
Teacher education	22.3	5.2	76.6	22.3	0.3	0.2
English and literature	22.0	9.7	73.1	24.2	0.3	0.4
Communications	17.7	10.2	61.4	11.6	0.3	0.9
Nursing	15.4	1.5	30.1	3.6	0.5	0.4
Computer sciences	15.0	3.5	65.4	12.3	0.2	0.3
Fine arts	8.1	8.5	42.0	16.8	0.2	0.5
Occupation programs	7.6	1.1	54.3	6.0	0.1	0.2
Average	36.0	13.5	74.8	19.0	0.5	0.7

both two-year versus four-year appointment and general field of instruction, are substantially less likely to hold these degrees.

The failure of the survey to include the M.F.A. as a terminal degree understates higher degrees in fine arts. Note also that degrees such as M.B.A.'s and M.P.A.'s were considered M.A.'s and are not included here. Specifically, only 36 percent of part-time faculty at four-year institutions have Ph.D.'s or professional degrees, compared to 74.8 percent of full-time faculty at four-year institutions. In two-year schools the proportion is 13.5 percent to 19.0 percent. Because this difference exists even controlling for level of institution, it raises serious questions about the assertion that part-time faculty are as qualified as full-time faculty. Table 5.3 breaks the Ph.D. rates down by VOC and LAC clusters.

No doubt some of the difference is due to the primary use of part-time faculty in four-year institutions to teach lower-division students. Nonetheless, the variances by level of institution and general field of instruction suggest that other factors are at work. The last two columns of Table 5.2 show the ratios of part-time to full-time faculty in four-year and two-year schools with higher degrees by general field of instruction. The ratio is higher in community colleges (.7 to 1) than four-year institutions (.5 to 1).

In several fields, including sociology, biology, health sciences, and communications, the two-year part-time faculty have proportions of Ph.D.'s or professional degrees similar to or higher than full-time faculty. It is not clear why two-year schools find a higher degree particularly appropriate in these fields. One possible explanation is that two-year colleges are pleased to employ faculty with higher degrees in fields where the rates they pay part-time faculty are apparently attractive as supplementary salaries for otherwise employed professionals. For reasons as yet unexplained, two-year colleges appear reluctant

Table 5.3. Proportion of Faculty with Higher Degrees by
Part-Time/Full-Time, Level of Institution, and Type of
Principal Teaching or Research Area

Level of Institution and Fields of Instruction or Research	Highest Degree					
	Percentage of Part-Time Faculty with Higher Degrees			Percentage of Full-Time Faculty with Higher Degrees		
	Ph.D.	Professional	Total	Ph.D.	Professional	Total
Four-Year Institutions:						
All	22.4	13.6	36.0	65.3	9.5	74.8
VOC cluster	18.5	29.3	47.8	57.2	18.5	75.7
LAC cluster	21.4	3.6	25.0	69.6	4.1	73.7
Two-Year Institutions:						
All	8.3	5.2	13.5	16.8	2.2	19.0
VOC cluster	12.7	9.4	22.1	11.0	3.2	14.2
LAC cluster	4.7	3.5	8.2	25.5	1.7	27.2

to compete for these faculty at the full-time market rate for fully supported professional staff.

The low proportion of four-year, part-time faculty with higher degrees in some fields, such as English and communications, compounds the high reliance on part-time faculty in these fields by four-year institutions. If the market is a factor here, it may cut both ways: lowering salaries in English and lowering hiring criteria in computer science where Ph.D.'s were formerly scarce. The generally low rate of Ph.D.'s for part-time four-year faculty in math, as well as English and communications, is especially disturbing in view of the widely noted "Ph.D. glut." Indeed, few liberal arts disciplines achieve even a 50 percent rate of Ph.D.'s for part-time faculty, despite Ph.D. rates of 88 to 94 percent of full-time faculty.

Attitudes of Part-Time Faculty

In view of the complex and unresolved variations in the use and professional preparation of part-time faculty by fields, the coherence in the attitudinal data in Table 5.4 is particularly striking. (This coherence may be modestly heightened, as initially intended, by the fact that the table, unlike the preceding table, includes only four-year faculty. Subsequent tables will, however, show similar disciplinary distinctions in two-year college, part-time faculty.) The twenty-four fields with sufficient response rates are ranked in accordance with the average part-time faculty satisfaction with their terms and conditions of employment. In all fields, overall satisfaction is substantially higher than satisfaction with salary, benefits, job security, or time to keep current in field.

The table highlights the eight most- and eight least-satisfied fields. The most-satisfied cluster includes the seven vocational fields and the physical sciences. The least-satisfied cluster includes the eight liberal arts fields. The clusters are not entirely homogeneous and the precise demarcations of the clusters would, of course, vary if one used the "job overall" or one of the specific employment issues to establish the ranking. Nonetheless, it is clear that part-time faculty in the VOC cluster are substantially more satisfied than part-time faculty in the LAC cluster. Although there is some overlap in the percentages at the margins for salary and benefits, the distinctions regarding job security and time to keep current in field are quite sharp. The concern for job security may reflect relative dependence on the part-time position but also has substantial implications for professional autonomy and academic freedom. The issue of time to keep current in field also raises profound professional concerns; those who teach the content of their jobs or professions feel more confident of their professional preparation than those whose part-time academic assignment may not reflect their principal endeavors or involvements.

Overall, the data indicate that between one- and two-thirds of four-year part-time faculty in the LAC cluster are dissatisfied with their specific terms and conditions of professional employment. In the remainder of this chapter, I will

Table 5.4. Teaching or Research Fields of Part-Time Faculty at Four-Year Institutions Who Are Satisfied with Their Employment

Teaching or Research Field	Percentage of Faculty Somewhat or Very Satisfied with:					Average Satisfaction
	Benefits	Salary	Job Security	Time to Keep Current in Field	Job Overall	
First-professional health	70.3	62.1	76.3	76.1	89.4	74.8
Nursing	59.1	69.3	62.7	69.1	96.7	71.4
Occupation programs	52.5	67.6	59.3	81.8	94.1	71.1
Law	51.9	58.1	65.6	82.4	93.9	70.4
Business	46.0	61.5	66.4	79.9	93.8	69.5
Engineering	58.0	55.7	53.3	82.8	91.7	68.3
Physical sciences	52.7	60.0	55.7	79.3	85.8	66.7
Teacher education	50.6	49.2	60.4	81.8	90.8	66.6
Other social science	56.0	57.7	53.6	71.7	91.2	66.0
Other education	47.1	52.9	67.3	67.4	92.4	65.4
Computer sciences	40.9	56.8	53.6	83.9	91.2	65.3
Mathematics and statistics	46.2	53.5	57.3	82.9	84.3	64.8
Other health science	41.8	54.1	63.3	73.2	86.8	63.8
Psychology	47.5	51.0	53.7	76.7	89.0	63.6
Communications	38.4	57.3	52.0	75.7	93.5	63.4
All other programs	46.0	55.1	55.2	70.3	83.7	62.1
Political sciences	50.8	69.7	33.2	66.8	82.2	60.5
Biological sciences	46.1	46.9	49.5	70.9	88.5	60.4
Philosophy and religion	40.3	55.9	46.4	60.3	71.7	54.9
Sociology	52.3	46.3	39.6	49.6	80.8	53.7
Fine arts	32.0	43.4	43.2	67.3	78.7	52.9
Foreign languages	31.9	43.9	33.2	63.3	82.4	50.9
English and literature	32.1	36.2	33.3	57.9	76.0	47.1
History	29.9	28.4	37.5	50.6	65.7	42.4
Average	45.2	52.4	54.2	72.1	86.3	62.0

Note: Rankings are in descending order of average satisfaction; economics and agriculture/economics omitted because of insufficient numbers.

explore this dissatisfaction and other differences between the LAC and VOC clusters in order to better understand the differences between these part-time faculty groups and to consider the implications of the differences for academic employment and educational policies.

Economic Condition of Part-Time Faculty

The duties of part-time faculty require professional training, ability, skills, and performance. Gappa and Leslie (1996) argue further that "unlike a typical dual labor market, in which the secondary employees are an economically vulnerable underclass, the part-time faculty work force is largely voluntary, reasonably well-off in economic terms, and professionally qualified for the work they do" (p. 12). The authors recognize that some part-time faculty may lack these characteristics but argue persuasively that part-time faculty are, on average, more similar to than different from their full-time counterparts. Accordingly, they conclude that it is only their substandard terms and conditions of employment, not their professional qualifications and orientation, that distinguish part-time faculty.

This argument is conceptually troubling. From an economic perspective, and indeed a commonsense one, it is counterintuitive to suppose that equally qualified individuals would voluntarily accept substandard working conditions. Yet the data in Table 5.4 do support the contention that an overwhelming majority—86 percent—of part-time faculty express overall satisfaction with their part-time employment. (Table 5.8, presented later in text, shows that a large majority also affirm their desire to participate in an academic environment, and a narrow majority affirm their preference for part-time status in their particular position.) Table 5.4 also confirms that many, even most, of these faculty express deep dissatisfaction with their poor wages and lack of benefits, job security, and opportunity for advancement.

We are left, therefore, with a need to explain why part-time faculty, seemingly voluntarily, accept terms and conditions of employment that are substantially less attractive than their apparently similarly qualified full-time colleagues. There is no single answer to this conundrum, but further consideration of the disaggregated part-time data suggests several useful explanations. We will begin with the question of professional qualifications.

To the extent that professional qualifications are understood in terms of academic ability, there is empirical support for the contention that part-time faculty are similar to their full-time counterparts. The data on undergraduate academic awards in Table 5.5 show that full-time faculty are slightly more likely to have earned undergraduate academic awards. Similarly, LAC faculty are marginally more likely than VOC faculty to have earned such awards. The pattern seems clear, and the small differences are not significant. So part-time faculty are statistically no less likely to have earned academic recognition as undergraduate students.

However, we already know from Table 5.2 that the professional preparation of part-time faculty is less advanced than that of their full-time colleagues,

**Table 5.5. Proportion of Full-Time and Part-Time Faculty at
Four-Year Institutions Earning Undergraduate Academic Awards
by Fields of Instruction or Research**

| | Undergraduate Awards | | | |
| | Graduation Cum Laude | | Any Undergraduate Academic Awards | |
Fields of Instruction or Research	Percentage Full-Time	Percentage Part-Time	Percentage Full-Time	Percentage Part-Time
VOC cluster	20.4	18.7	62.4	55.1
LAC cluster	22.3	20.3	64.8	58.1
All	19.4	19.4	63.6	56.5

as measured by level of advanced degrees. Controlling for level of institution and discipline, part-time faculty are about half as likely as their full-time counterparts to have Ph.D.'s or professional degrees.

When data in Table 5.2 are aggregated into the VOC and LAC groupings, significant variances based on level of institution and disciplinary clusters appear (tabulation omitted due to lack of space). Although the Ph.D. is more common in LAC disciplines, VOC part-time faculty are substantially more likely to have either a Ph.D. or a professional degree than LAC part-time faculty in both four-year and two-year institutions. LAC full-time faculty are about as likely as VOC full-time faculty to have these higher degrees in four-year institutions and more likely in two-year institutions. But most significantly, LAC part-time faculty are only about one-third (25/73.7 four-year and 8.2/27.2 two-year) as likely to have these degrees as LAC full-time faculty. In contrast, almost two-thirds (47.8/75.7) of VOC part-time faculty in four-year schools hold these higher degrees, and VOC faculty in two-year schools are nearly two-thirds (22.1/14.2) *more* likely to have these degrees. Overall then, VOC part-time faculty are significantly better professionally prepared and more like their full-time colleagues than LAC part-time faculty.

Nonetheless, most LAC part-time faculty engage in lower-division instruction where, some argue, a research degree is often superfluous. If we proceed on the basis that part-time faculty have evidenced comparable ability and that their degrees are at least appropriate to their professional responsibilities, what other factors might account for their acceptance of relatively disadvantageous terms of employment? Part of the answer lies in reexamining the claim that part-time faculty are not "an economically vulnerable underclass" and are "economically reasonably well-off."

Table 5.6 compares the economic circumstances of VOC and LAC part-time faculty in both four-and two-year institutions. If the average household income of part-time faculty is not that of an "economically vulnerable underclass," this is only because the poverty level income from the part-time position (column 1) from which they responded provided less than one-quarter of

Table 5.6. Income of Part-Time Faculty by Level of Institution and Field of Instruction or Research

Level of Institution and Fields of Instruction or Research	Average Income in Dollars by Type of Income		
	Academic Year Salary from Institution	Total Individual Income	Total Household Income
Four-Year Institutions:			
All	$11,560	$53,779	$74,278
VOC cluster	12,398	69,563	92,846
LAC cluster	11,719	38,508	58,858
Percent LAC of VOC	94.5	55.4	63.4
Two-Year Institutions:			
All	8,590	41,994	58,207
VOC cluster	7,399	51,748	63,511
LAC cluster	9,489	35,089	55,798
Percent LAC of VOC	128.2	67.8	87.9

their individual income (column 2) and one-fifth of their household income (column 3). Part-time wages are set in a market in which many of the participants are content to supplement income and benefits received elsewhere. We will consider later the implications of this dependence on outside income for professional performance.

The LAC faculty in four-year institutions, who averaged $38,508 annually, earned only 55 percent as much individual income as the VOC faculty. Even in two-year institutions, where the LAC faculty actually earned more income from their part-time positions, their individual income of $35,089 was only 68 percent that of VOC faculty. The fact that LAC part-time faculty are more dependent on their part-time positions helps explain the substantially greater discontent manifest by LAC faculty in Table 5.4, especially if one considers that a substantial group of LAC faculty have salaries and income well below the average.

This greater dependence of LAC part-time faculty is more directly evident in Table 5.7, which displays the proportion of part-time faculty who hold full- or part-time positions in addition to their teaching positions. Fewer than 25 percent of part-time faculty subsist solely on a single part-time position. LAC part-time faculty were, however, 40 to 50 percent more likely than VOC part-time faculty not to have an additional position. Moreover, LAC part-time faculty were about half as likely to hold a *full-time* additional position and twice as likely to have one or more additional *part-time* positions. These data help explain both the lower individual income and the greater concern for job security and benefits among LAC part-time faculty.

Because LAC faculty depend substantially more than VOC faculty on part-time employment, we need to consider the extent to which LAC part-time faculty "voluntarily" select part-time work. Table 5.8 summarizes the responses

**Table 5.7. Proportion of Part-Time Faculty
Who Hold Additional Employment by Type of Employment,
Level of Institution, and Field of Instruction or Research**

Level of Institution and Fields of Instruction or Research	Additional Full-Time Position	Additional Part-Time Position(s)	No Additional Position
Four-Year Institutions:			
All	44.1%	31.7%	24.2%
VOC cluster	57.8	22.2	20.0
LAC cluster	29.6	41.8	28.7
Ratio of LAC to VOC	0.5	1.9	1.4
Two-Year Institutions:			
All	50.3	28.3	21.4
VOC cluster	64.9	18.0	17.1
LAC cluster	36.0	38.5	25.5
Ratio of LAC to VOC	0.6	2.1	1.5

of part-time faculty at four-year institutions to several questions regarding their rationales for accepting part-time positions. The claim that the choice of part-time work is voluntary derives support from the 70 percent of four-year institution respondents, and almost as many LAC as VOC faculty, who said that they held part-time positions because they "wanted to be part of an academic environment." Similarly, over half of the respondents, including almost as many LAC as VOC faculty said they were "supplementing [their] income from other employment." Community college faculty responded quite similarly, although even more (63 percent) were supplementing their income from other employment.

Although about half of part-time faculty affirmed that they "preferred working on a part-time basis," VOC faculty were more than half again as likely to say this as were LAC faculty. Most significantly, three-fifths of both four-year and two-year LAC faculty—more than twice the proportion of VOC faculty—stated that they held part-time positions because "a full-time position was not available." Gender is also a significant variable here. Although women and men were similarly attracted to the academic environment, both VOC and LAC female part-time faculty were more likely to state that a full-time position was not available and not that they were supplementing their income. Two-year, male, part-time LAC faculty were more likely to share this perspective than their counterparts in four-year institutions. The greater proportion of women who affirm that they work part-time because full-time positions are unavailable seriously challenges those who argue that women particularly desire the flexibility of part-time appointments. In sum, though most part-time faculty do prefer working in academe, about three-fifths of LAC part-time faculty do not prefer part-time appointments and feel constrained to accept part-time positions.

Table 5.8. Selected Reasons Cited for Accepting Part-Time
Appointments by Level of Institution, Type of Principal
Teaching/Research Area and Gender

Did you hold a part-time position at this institution because:	All Disciplines % Yes			Cluster of Vocationally Oriented Fields % Yes			Cluster of Liberal-Arts Oriented Fields % Yes		
	All	Men	Women	All	Men	Women	All	Men	Women
Four-Year Institutions:									
You wanted to be part of an academic environment?	70.9	71.1	70.8	72.9	71.6	73.6	68.3	68.6	68.1
You preferred working on a part-time basis?	53.9	55.1	52.5	65.1	65.3	64.9	41.1	40.3	41.9
You were supplementing your income from other employment?	52.9	58.0	46.6	51.6	56.3	43.7	48.4	56.2	41.5
A full-time position was not available?	41.1	35.0	48.6	27.7	22.7	36.2	60.0	56.2	63.3
Two-Year Institutions:									
You wanted to be part of an academic environment?	70.6	70.7	70.6	72.9	70.7	77.8	70.6	73.8	67.8
You preferred working on a part-time basis?	49.8	51.2	48	57.8	56.9	59.9	38.8	40.3	37.4
You were supplementing your income from other employment?	62.6	70.3	52.6	65.2	68.5	58.1	55.3	65.3	46.8
A full-time position was not available?	47.5	42.8	53.5	37.8	35.1	43.5	62.9	61.7	63.8

Implications for Quality

The constraint experienced by some part-time faculty and the disadvantageous terms of part-time faculty employment do have consequences. Performance measures are not easy to construct from the available data, but we will consider two with important implications for student learning: the use of essay exams and the scheduling of office hours. Part-time faculty, who are generally paid on a class-hour basis rather than for a proportion of a full faculty position, do less in each of these areas than full-time faculty do; but LAC faculty do substantially more than VOC faculty.

Table 5.9 compares the use of essay mid-terms or finals by part-time and full-time two- and four-year faculty. Such exams normally entail substantially more out-of-class time for grading. VOC faculty, whether full- or part-time, are significantly less likely to require such exams than LAC faculty; this seems, therefore, to reflect customary disciplinary pedagogy rather than any short-coming on the part of VOC part-time faculty. Moreover, part-time faculty overall are only modestly less likely than full-time faculty to require these exams in both four- and two-year institutions.

LAC part-time faculty are, however, over 50 percent less likely to require essay exams than LAC full-time faculty. Some of this disparity may reflect the lower-division assignments of most LAC part-time faculty, but these assignments do include large numbers of composition courses. At the same time, substantially more LAC part-time faculty than VOC part-time faculty carry the generally uncompensated out-of-class burden of grading these exams. So LAC part-time faculty must choose between a less demanding but possibly inadequate pedagogy and engaging in unremunerated work. This could help explain why these faculty more often feel undercompensated.

The data on office hours in Table 5.10 show that VOC part-time faculty, in both two-year and four-year schools, are substantially more likely than LAC part-time faculty to report that they have no scheduled office hours. But both VOC and LAC part-time faculty are far less likely to schedule office hours than are their full-time counterparts. Because the office hours of part-time faculty are usually not remunerated and might require the part-time students as well as the part-time faculty member to make special visits to campus, this finding is not surprising. But it does raise serious concerns about the quality of student access to their part-time instructors. Here again, the LAC part-time faculty are more likely than the VOC part-time faculty to perform uncompensated work.

Significant Variations Among Part-Time Faculty

Each of the disciplinary clusters of part-time faculty approximates one of the two contrasting views of part-time faculty. The vocationally oriented part-time faculty conform in many respects to the idealized image of part-time faculty appointments. They are more likely to bring advanced preparation and, especially, their

Table 5.9. Comparison of the Use of Essay Mid-Term or Final Exams by Part-Time and Full-Time Faculty, Level of Institution, and Field of Instruction or Research

| Level of Institution and Fields of Instruction or Research | Essay Mid-Terms or Finals | | | | | |
| | % None | | % Some | | % All | |
	Full-Time	Part-Time	Full-Time	Part-Time	Full-Time	Part-Time
Four-Year Institutions:						
All	35.2	44.0	32.6	22.5	32.2	33.5
VOC cluster	47.8	46.7	27.6	23.1	24.9	27.2
LAC cluster	23.2	38.4	35.4	19.9	41.5	41.6
Two-Year Institutions:						
All	46.1	52.8	30.2	21.3	23.7	26.0
VOC cluster	56.6	59.0	27.4	21.7	16.0	19.3
LAC cluster	24.8	37.4	36.9	22.6	38.3	40.1

Table 5.10. Office Hours of Full-Time and Part-Time Faculty by Level of Institution and Field of Instruction or Research

Level of Institution and Fields of Instruction or Research	Regularly Scheduled Office Hours Per Week					
	None		One to Five		Six or More	
	Full-Time	Part-Time	Full-Time	Part-Time	Full-Time	Part-Time
Four-Year Institutions:						
All faculty	8.5	40.7	48.5	43.5	43.0	15.8
VOC cluster	11.0	47.4	41.5	36.0	47.5	16.7
LAC cluster	7.3	30.5	57.5	51.7	35.2	14.7
Two-Year Institutions:						
All faculty	3.3	57.9	49.7	31.8	47.0	10.4
VOC cluster	3.9	65.4	51.8	23.2	44.3	11.4
LAC cluster	1.9	49.7	49.7	40.3	48.5	10.0

daily nonacademic professional experience to the classroom. Their outside earnings subsidize their academic activity and permit them to work at wage rates below those in nonacademic markets. Similarly, they more often have full-time, nonacademic jobs that may provide greater job security and the security of insurance benefits. Their academic duties apparently require less out-of-class time for grading and office hours. Accordingly, they can enjoy the psychic benefits of academic involvement and make a professional contribution to their institutions, which most do not find substantially compromised by the terms and conditions of their part-time employment.

However, the liberal-arts-oriented cluster of part-time faculty are not only substantially more discontented but have substantial reasons for their discontent. These reasons include greater dependence on their part-time appointments, less job security, less availability of health or other fringe benefits, less satisfaction with part-time employment, lower individual and household income, and greater obligation to perform uncompensated work. These relative disadvantages do not include lower part-time earnings and may have some basis in the fact that LAC part-time faculty are less likely than VOC part-time faculty to have degrees beyond the master's. Yet because the LAC part-time faculty express greater professional concern about time to keep current in their fields and are more likely to require more demanding exams and uncompensated student access, equal pay may not, in fact, reflect equal work.

The fact that the instruction of entry-level students in the core liberal arts disciplines is heavily based on part-time teaching by an undercompensated and insecure staff certainly requires further exploration and concern. Pending such research, it seems fair to conclude that LAC part-time faculty feel constrained and economically vulnerable. Moreover, to the extent that they prefer academic work, they believe that they are forced by the lack of full-time positions and the need to accept a compensation structure set by the majority of part-time faculty who seek only supplemental income, to accept far less desirable part-time positions. Their dissatisfaction may be reflected in their diminished provision of office hours and use of essay exams relative to their full-time counterparts. Their insecurity may have even more serious implications for grading practices and academic freedom in the classroom. The issues here include not only fairness but also the educational consequences of shifting lower-division, liberal arts instruction to faculty who have negative performance incentives and lack the time and security essential for excellent instruction. Whatever their economic standing relative to nonacademic employees, as academic employees most LAC part-time faculty feel forced to accept terms and conditions of employment that do not ensure, and quite likely diminish, their academic performance.

Note

The total reported 1993 sample represents approximately 1,034,000 faculty, including 598,000 full-time (57.8 percent) and 436,000 part-time (42.2 percent). For this study, however, I have restricted the sample to those faculty or staff engaged in credit instruction who report teaching as their principal responsibility. This results in a subsample representing approximately 739,900 faculty, including 392,500 full-time (53.05 percent) and 347,400 part-time (46.95 percent). Of these the 471,350 faculty in four-year institutions included 61.9 percent full-time and 38.1 percent part-time; the 268,550 faculty in two-year institutions included 37.6 percent full-time and 62.41 percent part-time.

The samples underlying these estimates were not large enough to provide useful, statistically reliable data by specific disciplines or even for each of the twenty-six general fields. The VOC and LAC clusters are, however, based on samples large enough to produce reliable results. The LAC and VOC clusters, respectively, represented about 247,000 (33.4 percent) and 235,000 (31.8 percent) faculty of the 740,000 in the subsample. The Ns represented vary slightly from table to table due to response rate variance, and the standard errors depended on the N per item. But even fairly detailed breakdowns, such as the office hour data in Table 5.9, had standard errors ranging from 0.5 to 2.8, which were similar to those for the other tables using the clusters and low enough to assure the significance of substantial variations. The numbers in the cluster table were generally about those in Table 5.9: 291,550 four-year full-time faculty (96.9 VOC, 97.5 LAC); 179,800 four-year part-time (60.6 VOC, 56.7 LAC); 100,950 two-year full-time faculty (37.4 VOC, 29.7 LAC); and 167,600 two-year part-time faculty (52.5 VOC and 51.3 LAC).

Reference

Gappa, J. M., and Leslie, D. W. "Two Faculties or One? The Conundrum of Part-Timers in a Bifurcated Work Force," Inquiry no. 6 of the "New Pathways" Project of the American Association for Higher Education, Mar. 1996.

ERNST BENJAMIN is associate general secretary, American Association of University Professors, Washington, D.C.

Increasing proportions of science faculty are in non-tenure-track positions, resulting in change for faculty, students, and the quality of academic research.

Implications for Knowledge Production and Careers in Science

Catherine D. Gaddy

Researchers and practitioners in the academic fields of science, engineering, and related technology have much in common with their colleagues in the humanities, education, and other professional fields with respect to the appropriate roles of part-time and adjunct faculty in higher education. As a result most, if not all, of the considerations discussed by others in this volume apply to the science and engineering (S&E) fields. To complement and expand further on these considerations, implications for and perspectives from science will be discussed here.

Role of S&E in Higher Education

First, what role does S&E play in higher education? In 1996, just over 29 percent of U.S. freshmen chose S&E-related majors (Sax, Astin, Korn, and Mahoney, 1996), including 9.2 percent in the social sciences, 8.2 percent in engineering, 7.0 percent in the biological sciences, 2.6 percent in computer science, 1.8 percent in the physical sciences, and 0.5 percent in mathematics.

Thirty-three percent of baccalaureate degrees and 19 percent of master's degrees awarded in 1994 were in S&E fields (National Science Foundation, 1996b). Of doctorates awarded in the United States in 1995, 66 percent were in S&E fields (over 27,000), compared with 16 percent in education, 12 percent in humanities, and 6 percent in other professional fields (Henderson, Clarke, and Reynolds, 1996). S&E faculty members were 33 percent of all faculties in 1993 (U.S. Department of Education, 1993). Thus S&E represent a sizable share of students and faculty, particularly at the doctoral level.

Among S&E faculty, between 1993 and 1995 the percentages of those in tenured and tenure-track positions generally decreased, whereas the percentages in non-tenure-track and other categories generally increased (see Table 6.1) (National Science Foundation, 1996a; 1997). The shift from more permanent

Table 6.1. Tenure Status of Doctoral Scientists and Engineers Employed in Universities and Four-Year Colleges, 1993 and 1995

| | Tenured | | Not Tenured | | | | | |
| | | | In Track | | Not in Track | | Not Applicable | |
	1993	1995	1993	1995	1993	1995	1993	1995
Total S&E	55.5%	52.1%	18.1%	16.5%	9.0%	9.7%	17.4%	21.7%
All science	54.8	51.8	17.7	16.3	9.2	9.9	18.2	22.0
Computer & math	65.3	65.3	21.8	19.7	6.1	5.5	6.7	9.5
Life	47.2	44.8	17.7	17.1	11.6	12.2	23.4	25.9
Physical	56.0	47.7	14.2	11.5	9.1	9.9	20.7	31.0
Social	59.1	57.9	18.4	17.3	7.7	8.6	14.8	16.2
Engineering	61.0	54.2	20.8	18.2	7.3	7.9	10.9	19.7

and (at present) prestigious to less permanent and less prestigious types of positions appears to be taking place within the ranks of S&E. The 5 percent increase in two years of those "not in track" and "not applicable" (from 26.4 percent in 1993 to 31.4 percent in 1995 for total S&E) is particularly noteworthy, considering that these data are for the entire doctoral workforce and not just a cohort of new doctorates.

Careers in S&E

The proportion of doctoral scientists and engineers pursuing employment in academe has decreased, whereas the percentage of those in business and industry has increased. In 1995, fewer than half (46 percent) worked in universities and four-year colleges (National Science Foundation, 1997). Some percentage of S&E doctorates have always pursued jobs outside academe for most or all of their careers, particularly in fields such as chemistry and engineering. Recently, increasing percentages of their colleagues in the biological sciences, mathematics, and other physical sciences (for example, earth and space sciences and physics) have begun to pursue employment in business or industry or other nonacademic settings.

To some extent this shift in employment sector has probably been driven by the increase in production of doctorates, coupled with the decrease in tenure-track positions (a "push" away from academe). The shift may also have been influenced by the increase in sophisticated technology in business and industry, such as in the biotechnology and pharmaceutical, computer, consumer-products, petroleum, and telecommunications industries (a "pull" toward business and industry).

Meanwhile, consistently higher salaries in business and industry (National Science Foundation, 1997) are probably a strong lure for some scientists and engineers. At the same time, the opportunity to pursue research with (perhaps) greater freedom and to train the next generation of scientists in academe provides a pull toward higher education. Whatever the many and varied reasons for career choices throughout the life span, and whether voluntary or not, more scientists and engineers are working outside of academe than ever before. To some degree, the personnel policies and practices of higher education have less proximal influence on the careers of those who choose a nonacademic path. But the treatment of those who teach or train the next generation is still of concern to all scientists and citizens.

Further, scientists employed in business, industry, or other nonacademic settings encounter many of the same issues of job security and stability, as well as respect (or lack thereof) for one's contribution, that are encountered by academics. "Reengineering" has many faces and implications for individuals, institutions and organizations, and society. So some of what we learn about the uses and abuses of part-time and adjunct faculty will undoubtedly have ramifications for treatment of professionals in other sectors.

Trend Toward Less Certain Times

As shown in Figure 6.1, the percentage of all new doctorates who have definite plans at graduation has steadily declined since 1960 (Clarke, 1996). As seen in Table 6.1, this trend is evident across fields (Clarke, 1996). Further, among those graduates who do have plans, an increasing percentage are heading off to temporary postdoctoral positions; as many as 73 percent of 1995 bioscience doctoral students went to postdocs (Henderson, Clarke, and Reynolds, 1996). At the same

Figure 6.1. Doctorate Recipients with Definite Plans

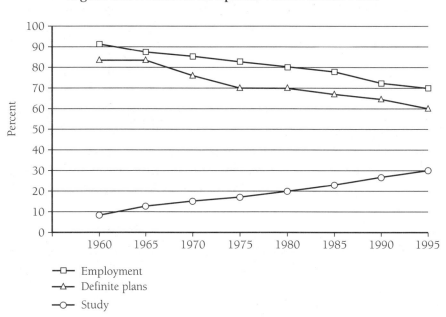

—□— Employment
—△— Definite plans
—○— Study

Table 6.2. Percentage of Doctoral Graduates with Definite Plans

	1960	1995
Physical sciences	86	59
Engineering	83	51
Life sciences	81	64
Social sciences	83	59
Humanities	84	54
Education	84	66

time, the numbers of recently graduated doctorate-holders going directly to employment have decreased. Thus the times are less certain for today's doctorate-holders than they were for the previous generation; more, primarily in S&E, are headed to temporary postdoctoral positions, which will require that they begin the job search again in two to four years.

According to a recent survey by the Association of American Universities, most of these postdocs expect tenure-track positions in research universities. Yet recent NSF data (Regets, 1997) show that of those in postdoctoral positions in 1993, only 13 percent were in tenure-track positions by 1995, and of those in second or more postdocs in 1993, only 16 percent were on a tenure track two years later. Not only are times less certain by some measures but they are likely to remain less certain for longer periods of time in the careers of many scientists and engineers.

As Regets (1997) notes, if some postdocs are taking multiple appointments while waiting for a tenure-track opening, not only might their odds of obtaining such a position be relatively low but they might unintentionally foreclose on other options. Anecdotal reports from employers in business and industry suggest that nonacademic employers may be hesitant to hire someone who has had multiple postdocs, wondering if this individual can function outside a university laboratory (where most postdocs are found).

Some who finish their postdocs, as well as other recent graduates, are taking adjunct or part-time positions as a "foot in the door" and to get teaching experience. Here again, it would be helpful for these part-time and temporary faculties to know the odds of transitioning to a more permanent position.

These changes in the predictability of one's career may be structural ones that are necessary for global competitiveness (as suggested by Tobias, Chubin, and Aylesworth, 1995). But how much insecurity and instability is healthy, either for individuals or institutions? Seemingly, candidates for science careers have appeared in unending supply from home and abroad, yet what does this lack of permanence and certainty do to the long-range attractiveness of science as a field of study and as a career? When new doctorates or postdocs do land jobs that are involuntarily part-time (perhaps without benefits) or as adjuncts, what message does this send to scientists and the broader community about the extent to which we value scientific knowledge?

Given the increased uncertainty of the times, faculty advisers should guide their students toward diverse opportunities that will use their skills and knowledge. Will advisers feel compelled to warn promising students away from academic jobs if the positions are perceived as less stable or mainstream (adjunct) or less rewarding (part-time, perhaps without benefits)? Will promising graduates attempt a career in the professoriate, only to find an adjunct role and then leave for more fulfilling and rewarding employment elsewhere?

Effects on Achievements and Productivity. Because 13 percent of the nation's total research and development (R&D) budget is invested in academic institutions (Teich, 1996), what are the consequences for this important share of R&D, given the changing landscape of higher education? Few part-time or adjunct faculties are likely to be engaged in university-based research, at least to the same extent as their full-time or "permanent" colleagues.

If some part-timers or adjuncts are classic part-timers—defined by Rajagopal and Lin (1996) as someone having a full-time nonacademic job in addition to teaching part-time—these individuals can infuse different experiences, such as those from industrial laboratory settings, that can be quite valuable and perhaps increase productivity. And communications can be two-way, with the part-time academic taking new insights back to a full-time, nonacademic job.

Some academic part-timers may also be part-time caregivers; they may be transitioning to retirement or another career path, volunteering in their communities, or engaging in some other pursuit. In these instances a more fulfilled person may result—one who can communicate the potential flexibility of science careers to others in similar situations.

However, the contemporary part-timers are of concern—*contemporaries* being defined by Rajagopal and Lin (1996) as those attempting to make a career of one or more part-time positions, often with low pay, no benefits, and little camaraderie—particularly if the new generation of doctorates is disproportionately represented among these ranks. We need not hearken back to Maslow's theories to remind ourselves that it is quite difficult to (in his terminology) "self-actualize" in the pursuit of creative research and the generation of new knowledge when one is worried about the more basic ("lower-level") needs for food and shelter.

Other Effects of Part-Time Employment. A relatively small percentage of all scientists and engineers work on a part-time basis for their principal employment (5.7 percent in 1995; National Science Foundation, 1997). However, it seems that at the heart of the institutional and societal concern over part-time and adjunct faculty is the issue of quality rather than quantity of time employed per se. Is the quality of part-time and adjunct faculty the same as for full-time, permanent faculty?

Klein, Weisman, and Smith (1996) conducted an exploratory study of eight social work programs; their findings indicated that students regarded adjunct faculty as somewhat less effective teachers than full-time faculty but appreciated their expertise on contemporary or specialized practices. Whether these findings can be generalized to other fields and whether the losses in teaching effectiveness were offset by the gains in knowledge from nonacademic settings remains to be determined. Not surprisingly, higher education administrators report that they appreciate the financial savings and flexibility associated with the use of adjunct instructors. The adjuncts themselves appreciate the affiliation with academic programs.

Are we in fact giving too little attention to the quality of the educational experience when we focus on job status labels such as *part-time* or *adjunct* versus *full-time* or *permanent,* when at least some of our focus should be on the quality of instruction or research? Given the challenges of measuring quality or productivity (see Klein, Wiseman, and Smith, 1996), it is difficult to determine the extent to which students are either benefiting or being deprived by exposure to part-time or adjunct faculty.

Effects of Federal Funding. A unique aspect of graduate education in science and engineering is the extent to which federal funds support research and education. A relatively small percentage of those in the humanities receive federal funding in the form of contracts or grants (6 percent in 1995, according to Ingram and Brown, 1997). The influence of federal dollars in S&E research and education is substantially greater, with 28 percent of doctoral scientists and engineers in the United States receiving federal support in the form of a contract or grant in 1995 (National Science Foundation, 1997).

Federal funds from the National Science Foundation (NSF), the National Institutes of Health (NIH), the National Aeronautics and Space Administration (NASA), the Department of Energy (DOE), and the Department of Defense (DOD) provide fellowships, traineeships, and research grants. The grants support faculty doing research and students working as research assistants, postdocs, or in similar roles. As a result, citizens (taxpayers) and others may rightfully question the allocation of public funds. Suppose an academic researcher turns over teaching responsibilities to an adjunct or part-timer so he can complete grant- or contract-supported research (and proposals for such). Is this an acceptable trade-off for the resultant research, or are the science students in the classrooms or laboratories being deprived of the knowledge of the experienced researcher?

Advantages and Disadvantages of Temporary Employment. Some of the advantages and disadvantages for the individual, institution, and society of an increase in the temporary nature of jobs and a concomitant decrease in job permanence are summarized in Table 6.3.

The trade-offs in individual and corporate decision making about temporaries versus permanent employees must be made for science and engineering, for other fields in higher education, and for the overall workforce.

Table 6.3. Advantages and Disadvantages of Temporary Work

	Potential Advantages	Potential Disadvantages
Individual	Opportunities for many interesting reasearch, teaching, or other assignments in parallel or sequentially	Less job security and stability Less commitment to specific lines of work or research
Institution or organization	Flexibility to hire and change staffing as needed Flexibility to have influx of ideas from new people	Less stability for and loyalty to the institution or organization
Society	Potential for increased competitiveness in global economy	Less clearly defined cadre of practiced talent in science and engineering fields of national interest

Summary and Recommendations

The use of part-time and other flexible workweek schedules can be beneficial in meeting individual and departmental needs. The use of adjuncts or other temporary positions also can provide specific skills, knowledge, and experience in the classroom or laboratory; it can provide occasional coverage of a course while recruiting for a permanent faculty position is under way.

Many of the reported abuses of the use of part-time or adjunct status (for example, Hardigg, 1995) seem to occur when individuals, particularly new doctorate-holders, are trying to make a living and launch a career by taking one or more temporary positions—the contemporary part-timers described earlier. This situation is not voluntary in the sense that it is preferred by the temporary faculty member.

I offer recommendations for improving this situation, some of which echo those suggested in other chapters:

Faculty advisers should provide students, especially graduate students and postdocs, with data on recent competition for permanent faculty positions (for example, Commission on Professionals in Science and Technology, 1997), as well as options for employment in diverse settings (for example, http://www.nextwave.org).

Academic departments should report the number of applicants for faculty positions. These data could then be publicized as one indicator of the competition (for example, Ralston, 1996).

Academic departments should review their roster of part-time or temporary employees. For those who are contemporaries, they should either provide career counseling themselves or in conjunction with campus career services and Internet resources. Contemporary part-timers also should know the realistic chances of securing a more permanent position with the employing institution.

Departments should track outcomes of their graduates (longitudinally) on some periodic basis to provide feedback to themselves and current students and to provide networking opportunities among current students and program alumni (for example, http://gsbs.gs.uth.tmc.edu/alumni/87survey/87survey.html).

Professional societies should provide data on employment outcomes of recent doctorates (cross-sectional). They have a clear interest in serving these potential new members and in carrying out the professional responsibility of assessing current job market conditions and the health of the field. Seed money for developing consistent and timely data collection and dissemination for S&E fields is being provided by the Commission on Professionals in Science and Technology project, in conjunction with professional societies and sponsored by Burroughs Wellcome Fund, National Science Foundation, and the Alfred P. Sloan Foundation (http://www.nextwave.org/; http://www.nextwave.org/survey1.htm). Two core questions in the survey are whether a part-time position was accepted because full-time was not available and whether a temporary job was accepted because a permanent one was not available.

Graduate students and doctorates should keep abreast of the changing job market via faculty, colleagues, Internet, and other formal (for example, http://www.nextwave.org) and informal resources.

Colleges and universities undoubtedly need flexibility to compete as the businesses they are. It is encouraging that this volume provides an opportunity for academic insiders and outsiders to debate trade-offs between flexible business practices and reasonable employee management.

References

Clarke, J. E. "Selected Data from the Doctoral Records File." Unpublished data, National Research Council, Washington, D.C., 1996.

Commission on Professionals in Science and Technology. *Postdocs and Career Prospects: A Status Report.* Washington, D.C.: Commission on Professionals in Science and Technology, 1997.

Hardigg, V. "Gypsy Profs: They are Underemployed Academics Who Find They Must String Together Teaching Posts." *U.S. News & World Report,* Mar. 20, 1995, p. 106.

Henderson, P. H., Clarke, J. E., and Reynolds, M. A. *Summary Report 1995: Doctorate Recipients from United States Universities.* Washington, D.C.: National Academy Press, 1996.

Ingram, L., and Brown, P. *Humanities Doctorates in the United States: 1995 Profile.* Washington, D.C.: National Academy Press, 1997.

Klein, W. C., Weisman, D., and Smith, T. E. "The Use of Adjunct Faculty: An Exploratory Study of Eight Social Work Programs." *Journal of Social Work Education,* 1996, 32 (2), 253–263.

National Science Foundation. *Characteristics of Doctoral Scientists and Engineers in the United States: 1993.* Arlington, Va.: National Science Foundation, 1996a.

National Science Foundation. *Science and Engineering Degrees, by Race/ethnicity of Recipients, 1987–1994.* Arlington, Va.: National Science Foundation, 1996b.

National Science Foundation. *Characteristics of Doctoral Scientists and Engineers in the United States: 1995.* Arlington, Va.: National Science Foundation, 1997.

Rajagopal, I., and Lin, Z. "Hidden Careerists in Canadian Universities." *Higher Education,* 1996, *32* (3), 247–266.

Ralston, A. "The Demographics of Candidates for Faculty Positions in Computer Science." *Communications of the ACM,* 1996, *39* (3), 78–84.

Regets, M. "1995 NSF Data on Labor-market Conditions for New Ph.D. Recipients," 1997. http://www.nextwave.org; http://www.nextwave.org/server-java/SAM/pastfor/nsf.htm.

Sax, L. J., Astin, A. W., Korn, W. S., and Mahoney, K. M. *The American Freshman: National Norms for Fall 1996.* Los Angeles, Calif.: Higher Education Research Institute, University of California, 1996.

Teich, A. H. "An Introduction to R&D in the Federal Budget." In Intersociety Working Group (ed.), *AAAS Report XXI, Research and Development FY 1997.* Washington, D.C.: American Association for the Advancement of Science, 1996.

Tobias, S., Chubin, D. E., and Aylesworth, K. *Rethinking Science as a Career: Perceptions and Realities in the Physical Sciences.* Tucson, Ariz.: Research Corporation, 1995.

U.S. Department of Education. *1993 National Study of Postsecondary Faculty.* Washington, D.C.: U.S. Department of Education, 1993.

CATHERINE D. GADDY is executive director of the Commission on Professionals in Science and Technology, Washington, D.C.

Splitting tenure-track and other faculty into separate departments changes conditions of participation in the academic enterprise.

Two-Tiered Faculty Systems and Organizational Outcomes

Pamela S. Tolbert

Many higher education institutions lack systematic organizational procedures for selecting, evaluating, and retaining or releasing non-tenure-track faculty[1] (Leslie, Kellams, and Gunne, 1982; Gappa, 1984; Gappa and Leslie, 1993). The organizational consequences are not difficult to foresee. Because few institutions are willing to devote resources to recruitment for non-tenure-track positions, departments are forced to select faculty for such positions from an idiosyncratically generated pool of applicants. Without formal selection criteria, hiring is apt to be strongly influenced by personalistic factors. Furthermore, without regular systems of performance evaluation, decisions about whether to retain faculty or not must be based on restricted information. The limitations of typical personnel arrangements for non-tenure-track faculty, in combination with the very difficult working conditions (for example, last-minute hiring that precludes sufficient course preparation, minimal staff support for organizing course materials, assignment of faculty to overcrowded offices, and so forth), threaten institutions' ability to deliver high-quality education.

An increasing number of books and articles have attempted to spell out "good" organizational practices for employment of part-time and non-tenure-track faculty (Biles and Tuckman, 1986; Berver, Kurtz, and Orton, 1992; Bianco-Mathis and Chalofsky, 1996). However, whether these recommended practices can resolve problems in the employment of such faculty or whether deeper problems are associated with a two-tier employment system for faculty remains an open question.

In this chapter, I present a case study of a department at a large research university in which the use of nontenured faculty increased dramatically over three decades. I begin by examining the historical sources of the expansion. I describe the arrangements that were implemented to resolve these problems. These arrangements exemplify many of the "best management practices" for non-tenure-track faculty mentioned earlier. Based on discussions with non-tenure-track and tenure-track department members and university administrators, I assess the effectiveness of these employment arrangements in resolving problems and the general consequences for the department of having a large contingent of non-tenure-track faculty.

In concluding, I draw general implications from this case for organizational policy and practice involving non-tenure-track faculty. I also consider a variety of questions raised for further research on the organizational consequences of the employment of non-tenure-track faculty—questions to which educational and organizational researchers have provided surprisingly few empirical answers.

Non-Tenure-Track Faculty at a Research University: A Case Study

This case study illustrates organizational responses to a changing mix of faculty.

Department History. Up until a few years ago, teaching modern languages at the university was part of the domain of a single department—the Department of Linguistics and Foreign Languages (LFL). The department was composed of professorial faculty who specialized in linguistics and modern language studies and lecturers who were responsible for teaching introductory- and intermediate-level language classes. The use of lecturers to teach modern languages began at the university in the years following World War II; initially, lecturers were responsible for teaching "labs" (small classes that met four days a week and emphasized conversational skills), while professorial faculty organized the labs and delivered weekly lectures to the set of labs that were associated with a course.

Over time, language teaching at the undergraduate level, including the weekly lectures, was increasingly delegated to teaching assistants and lecturers. This delegation was, in large part, a function of a very high demand by undergraduates for language courses, created by the foreign language requirement of the college. Because enrollments in language classes were limited for pedagogical reasons, it became necessary to create a large number of classes and sections for courses like elementary Spanish and French. Staffing all these classes with full-time, tenure-track faculty was not considered economically feasible.

Course offerings of relatively rare languages also proliferated over time, due in part to the establishment of research centers whose funding was contingent on the teaching of particular foreign languages. Limited demand for these courses also made staffing them with full-time faculty problematic. Consequently, instruction in introductory language courses increasingly became the domain of teaching assistants and lecturers.

A number of years ago, the faculty decided that very heavy involvement of graduate students in teaching language classes was not in the best interests of either the undergraduates or the graduate instructors. The result was the further expansion of the number of lecturers employed by the language program. As the number of lecturers grew, so did their acknowledged dissatisfaction with their employment arrangements. Complaints included inadequacies of the procedures used for hiring and making personnel decisions, perceived pay inequities, lack of power in departmental decisions about the curriculum and management of the language, and general relations with the higher-status professorial faculty.

Unlike the latter group of faculty, which had a faculty council to serve as its agent in university decision making and problem solving, there were no official mechanisms or organizations responsible for handling lecturers' grievances. Promotion practices for lecturers became especially conflict-laden as the number of lecturers eligible for promotion in the department rose rapidly over time. Although the department had established promotion paths for lecturers, with specified criteria and procedures for promotion, many lecturers felt that these policies were not consistently applied and that promotion processes were unduly influenced by inappropriately informal criteria. These problems gave rise to increasingly open expression of dissatisfaction with working conditions among many lecturers, along with an exponential increase in the number of complaints filed by lecturers with the administration. The possibility of seeking bargaining status through union certification was discussed.

The administration repeatedly asked LFL to deal with these complaints but the problems were not resolved. A number of factors are likely to have contributed to the lack of effective action by the department. One was the low status traditionally ascribed to the more applied area of language teaching, indicated in part by the comparatively low educational credentials required of language teachers. A substantial number of lecturers had no formal graduate education and some had not received a baccalaureate. Even today, the main criterion for employment is proficiency in a given language, although increasing emphasis is being placed on possession of relevant graduate degrees and demonstrated knowledge of appropriate pedagogy.

Many of the prominent linguists in the department did not view modern language teaching as a substantive academic specialization or as an area to which the department should allocate scarce resources. In addition, although the tenure-track faculty enjoyed the resources that the language courses brought to the department, their distance from this area of teaching provided little motivation to devote time and energy to dealing with difficult governance issues involving lecturers. And finally, norms of academia, which emphasize the autonomy of individual faculty for managing teaching responsibilities, may also have contributed to a general reluctance and lack of preparation among professorial faculty to work collaboratively with lecturers.

Over time, mediating complaints and problems generated by lecturers in modern languages took up an increasing proportion of the associate dean's time, absorbing far more attention than any other unit in the Arts College. The department's inability to resolve the problems finally precipitated the administrative decision to split LFL into two departments—Foreign Language Studies

(FLS) and the Department of Linguistics. All of the lecturers were made members of FLS, along with a number of tenured and tenure-track faculty members who responded to the administration's invitation for those interested in language teaching to join the new department. At present, there are approximately sixty-five lecturers in the FLS and fewer than ten tenured or tenure-track faculty.

Current Organizational Arrangements for Lecturers. The arrangements now in place for the employment of lecturers in the department exemplify many of the standard recommendations for personnel practices involving non-tenure-track faculty. Lecturers are hired on renewable term contracts. They are first hired on a probationary contract, typically for one year, and their performance during the probationary period is assessed by departmental committees. If the assessment is positive, they are usually offered a three-year contract and, finally, a five-year contract. Although the former LFL had instituted promotion policies for lecturers, the lack of specificity and detail in these policies had been one of the key sources of conflict and dissatisfaction among lecturers. The procedures now in place in FLS are much more elaborated and carefully formalized.

· The length of the employment contract is linked to faculty rank as either lecturer or senior lecturer. Senior lecturers normally have taught at the college level for at least six years and must be recommended by the department for promotion, based on a peer review not only of their teaching performance but of their service work—contributions as undergraduate advisers, service through committee work, participation in developing the curriculum, and so forth. University policies now prescribe that lecturers who have been appointed for at least three years be given one-year advance notice of termination.

A few faculty are still hired as teaching associates or visiting lecturers (explicitly temporary positions), but fewer hold such positions than in the old LFL. Most lecturers are hired on a full-time basis; if that is not possible, the department tries to hire people for at least 50 percent time so they are eligible to receive benefits. The teaching load for full-time lecturers is three courses per semester. To qualify for full-time status, lecturers must sometimes teach multiple languages (for example, several sections of Spanish, along with a section of Tagalog). Professorial faculty normally teach two courses each semester but also have responsibility for research.

Lecturers receive many of the same benefits as regular faculty. Compensation policies are based on equity considerations, and many senior lecturers receive relatively generous salaries (comparable to those of many assistant and associate professors in the university). On average, however, lecturers' salaries are noticeably lower than those of tenure-track faculty, and the benefits they receive that are tied to salary levels (for example, retirement and life insurance) are also generally lower. Some research support (for example, funding for attending professional meetings) is available for senior lecturers, according to university policy, although at a lower level than professorial faculty receive. FLS has established a departmental fund to provide similar levels of support for lecturers as well. Recently, a university-level committee recommended provision of funded leaves to nonprofessorial faculty for professional development, but this policy has not yet been implemented.

Last year, the department responded to pressures from the administration by elaborating formal review standards and procedures for senior lecturers. These provide the basis for discipline and dismissal, as well as for merit awards. The administration originally asked to have such reviews done annually, but when faced with strenuously made arguments about the amount of administrative work required, they finally settled on ten-year reviews. In effect, most senior lecturers will thus be subject to review two or three times in the course of their employment. Many senior lecturers in the department were concerned about these reviews (in much the same way that tenured faculty are often concerned about post-tenure reviews). Implementation of the procedures and reviews have resulted in some dissatisfaction among senior lecturers who received unsatisfactory evaluations, but in the main, most view the current system as more equitable and less subject to idiosyncratic influences than the arrangements under LFL.

Organizational Outcomes. Although significant efforts have been made to include lecturers as full-fledged members of the department, and the formalization and clarification of hiring and review procedures is seen as a major improvement over past practices, there is still ongoing tension between lecturers and professorial faculty. In part, this tension is probably a residual effect of earlier relations between professorial staff and lecturers in LFL and may simply take time to dissipate. Unfortunately, some of the old tensions were refueled soon after FLS was created because economic pressures at the university led to a reduction in the number of lecturers and, concomitantly, to increases in class sizes. Originally, it was proposed that classes be expanded from twelve to twenty; after some negotiation, course enrollment was capped at fifteen. As a result of this, most probationary and short-term lecturers were not rehired. Although none of the positions of longer-term lecturers were eliminated, concerns about job security continue to be very salient to many lecturers, and this contributes to perceptions of a we-them division between those who are eligible for tenure and those who are not.

An additional complication to the establishment of smooth faculty relations arose at about the same time the LFL was split into two departments. The faculty council of the university, concerned about potential exploitation of lecturers on campus, passed a resolution making lecturers a part of the faculty, and giving them voting rights in departmental issues "directly related to their roles within the college or school and within the department." The legislation did not, however, offer specific guidelines for determining how to define such issues. In consequence, the legislation has not resolved disputes between tenure-track faculty and lecturers over decision-making rights and responsibilities and may have actually fueled new ones.

Nevertheless, both faculty groups feel that there are a number of substantial advantages to the university's arrangements for teaching modern languages over assignment of such courses to teaching assistants. Lecturers are often more motivated to perform well as teachers because of their long-term investment in the role; teaching assistants are more apt to treat such work as a short-term "dues-paying" part of their graduate education. Moreover, because of their ongoing involvement in language instruction, lecturers are both more willing and able to contribute to course planning. The decreased reliance by FLS on visiting lecturers and teaching associates is also viewed as having had a positive impact on the quality of teaching because, in the past, many instructors were hired at the last minute with little provision for class preparation or general orientation to the department and to teaching.

Although there is still friction between professorial and lecturer faculty members, changes in policies *have* helped to reduce lecturers' general dissatisfaction with their relationships with professorial colleagues. Also, most recognize the comparatively advantaged employment position of lecturers in the university relative to those in other institutions.

The large number of lecturers in the department has also had an impact on FLS's hiring of tenure-track faculty. Because professorial faculty are responsible for working closely with lecturers in a given language area and helping to manage the organization of the language classes, evidence of a real concern with the practical issues of providing language instruction and the ability to handle interpersonal and administrative issues in program provision have become important criteria in professorial-level hiring and promotion processes.

Because program administration takes up a substantial portion of professorial faculty's time, it is not clear that they have enough time for research. Nonetheless, promotion to tenure is still based on traditional academic criteria that give heavy weight to research performance: publications, grants, and peer evaluations. The two untenured professors in the department who were recently hired had each developed reasonably strong track records of research; thus, their ability to meet tenure criteria seemed likely at the time of their hiring. Whether brand new Ph.D.'s normally could manage starting a research program while also administering the language programs is unclear.

Organizational Implications

Although the empirical generalizability of any case study is subject to question, the initial reluctance of LFL to institute employment arrangements that were accepted by lecturers as equitable and consistent certainly parallels the observed failure of many institutions to implement such systems for non-tenure-track faculty. Hence, this case may offer some useful insights into the reasons for general organizational resistance to rationalizing and formalizing employment arrangements for this set of faculty, as well as the consequences of such resistance. Although the fact that the department was part of a large research university might suggest that any conclusions should be limited to other research universities, there is little reason to suspect that the tensions that affect the relationship between tenure-track and non-tenure-track faculty in this context are any less likely to arise in other institutions.

What conclusions can be drawn for other institutions? First, *implementing systematic procedures for making decisions regarding the hiring and continued employment of non-tenure-track faculty is critical to maintaining good relations among tenure-track and non-tenure-track faculty in a department—relations that can affect a department's ability to provide high-quality education.* Employing faculty on a casual basis without minimal levels of instructional support severely limits the ability of even the most talented and motivated individuals to present subject matter in an organized and intellectually engaging manner (Gappa, 1984; Gemmill, 1984; Pratt, 1997).

What is not usually acknowledged is that non-tenure-track faculty are often inclined to attribute negative experiences of their employment situation to the tenure-track faculty and to view them, at best, as self-absorbed and insensitive and, at worst, as intentionally exploitative. This, in turn, is likely to have an impact on the overall quality of teaching in a department because divisions within the faculty can impede the sharing of experiences and knowledge that enhance individuals' teaching performance and limit flows of information that are needed to improve or develop the curriculum. In addition, unpleasant and contentious collegial relations can impede teaching performance by affecting faculty morale and motivation. Thus, more elaborated and formalized procedures and criteria for hiring and evaluating the performance of non-tenure-track faculty can reduce general dissatisfaction with the employment situation and contribute to the effective accomplishment of a department's educational function.

Second, *professorial faculty are unlikely to initiate organizational procedures for hiring, evaluating, and making decisions about continuing employment of non-tenure-track faculty.* There are entirely rational reasons for this lack of initiative. First, as long as positions are subject to elimination by administrative fiat, efforts to create and implement careful selection and evaluation procedures may turn into wasted expenditures of time and energy. Moreover, there is a strong disincentive to develop systematic personnel procedures for non-tenure-track faculty, because the development of such procedures can make the practice of using non-tenure-track faculty increasingly credible and justifiable, thus weakening faculty's claims for additional tenure-track positions.

Third, *the establishment of systematic employment procedures for non-tenure-track faculty is likely to require active administrative sponsorship.* Although faculty may be reluctant to devote time to creating and implementing formal employment criteria, they are clearly in a better position to determine the criteria for selection of fellow faculty in a given field and to evaluate teaching performance. Therefore, the administration should be prepared to offer incentives to faculty to undertake such activity. Positive incentives (in the form of additional compensation or release time from other activities for such administrative work) are more likely to produce better outcomes than empty appeals or threats. In addition, because faculty are sensitive to the potential costs of validating the use of non-tenure-track positions by rationalizing employment arrangements, the administration should work with faculty to develop policy concerning the absolute number of non-tenure-track positions for a department, or even better, the ratio of tenure-track to non-tenure-track positions in a department and in the institution as a whole.

Fourth, *waiting until there is a critical mass of non-tenure-track faculty before trying to formalize and implement organizational procedures involving such faculty is a strategic administrative error.* Consistent with some of the more general research on organizational demography (for example, South, Bonjean, Markham, and Corder, 1982; Tolbert, Simons, and Andrews, 1995), the case suggests that the presence of a large number of non-tenure-track faculty in a department contributes to the development and entrenchment of a strong sense of we-them division. The substantial increase in the proportion of lecturers in the department was the result of policies adopted both by the university and the original LFL without careful consideration of the staffing arrangements that would be necessitated or the degree to which these arrangements would be very counterproductive to collaborative relations. Because the increased use of non-tenure-track faculty in many institutions is likely to be less a result of fully analyzed, strategic decisions than of efforts to adapt to immediate exigencies, administrators or faculty are unlikely to anticipate the potential divisions between tenure-track and non-tenure-track faculty.

However, once generated, such divisions take their toll on departmental relations, even after the material conditions that may have been associated with such divisions are changed. Recognition of the general effects of departmental composition on group relations led some members interviewed for the case study (including some lecturers) to argue strongly for policies that set close limits on the relative proportion of lecturers in a department. But it is not clear that policies alone can completely forestall such divisions. The proportionate make-up of different groups of faculty may well have an independent effect on the ability of the department to come to consensus.

Long-Term Implications

Although the pros and cons of the use of non-tenure-track faculty have long been the subject of heated debate (see, for example, O'Toole, Van Alstyne, and Chait, 1979), empirical evidence on the long-term organizational consequences of such use is surprisingly sparse. We know very little about what effect the increasing use of non-tenure-track faculty might have in the short- or long-term on the stability of revenue-expenditure balances, revenues from grants and contracts, changes in tuition rates, institutional prestige and reputation, and other organizational outcomes. Although logical arguments support claims that tenure systems are both economically efficient (McPherson and Winston, 1988; Carmichael, 1988; Ehrenberg, Pieper, and Willis, 1995), and inefficient (Chait and Ford, 1982), empirical data have not been used to test and verify these claims. Hence, there is clearly an important need for more systematic research on the actual outcomes for higher education institutions of relying more or less on heavily on non-tenure-track faculty.

Perhaps more troublesome potential outcomes involve the occupational effects of growth in the number of non-tenure-track faculty. One potential outcome, which has often been alluded to in studies of non-tenure-track faculty (see American Association of University Professors, 1992; Rhoades, 1996; Tolbert, 1997), is the deinstitutionalization of tenure as an employment system. To argue that academic freedom must be protected for those involved in the generation of new knowledge, but not for those who are involved exclusively or largely in the transmission of knowledge, does not seem defensible. Thus on logical grounds (versus purely economic grounds), unless tenure is provided for all long-term faculty members, its necessity and legitimacy is problematic. But the empirical support for such logical arguments is lacking. One possible approach to exploring whether the use of non-tenure-track faculty is indeed likely to lead to the de-legitimation of tenure is to examine whether the proportion of non-tenure-track faculty in institutions at one point in time affects changes in the proportion at later time points. A significant positive effect, net of other influences, could be taken as an indicator of the deinstitutionalization of the tenure system.

A common concern expressed by proponents of tenure is that without such an employment arrangement, the ability of the academic profession in the United States to attract men and women of sufficient caliber to maintain the current national preeminence among higher education systems would decline sharply. Although changes in labor professional markets occur very slowly (Freidson, 1994), the impact of the elimination of tenure-track positions on entry into the profession might be gauged by systematic comparison of the rates of application and the quality of graduate applicants in fields where there has been a trend to a high ratio of non-tenure-track positions with those in fields where non-tenure-track positions have been less common.

In sum, the short-term negative organizational outcomes that can accompany the employment of faculty in non-tenure-track positions can probably be minimized by implementing preventive personnel policies *before* conflicts arise. However, the actual economic and reputational outcomes to an institution that arise over the long run from the employment of non-tenure-track faculty are more difficult to assess in the absence of systematic research. In the longer term, the implications for higher education of the decline of tenure, which are foreshadowed by the increasing use of non-tenure-track faculty, are both elusive and problematic. Such long-term issues merit much more extensive research as a basis for informed and effective policy.

Note

1. I prefer the term *non-tenure-track* to *part-time* faculty because it defines more precisely the group that is of concern to most analysts. I also use the term *professorial faculty* to designate tenure-track faculty, based on conventional ranks for such faculty (assistant professor, associate professor, and so forth).

References

American Association of University Professors, Committee G. "Report on the Status of Non-Tenure-Track Faculty. *Academe,* 1992, Nov./Dec., 39–48.

Berver, K., Kurtz, D., and Orton, E. "Off the Track, but in the Fold. *Academe,* Nov./Dec. 1992, 27–29.

Bianco-Mathis, V., and Chalofsky, N. *The Adjunct Faculty Handbook.* Thousand Oaks, Calif.: Sage, 1996.

Biles, G., and Tuckman, H. *Part-time Faculty: Personnel Management.* New York: Macmillan, 1986.

Carmichael, L. "Incentives in Academics: Why is there Tenure? *Journal of Political Economy,* 1988, *96* (4), 453–472.

Chait, R., and Ford A. *Beyond Traditional Tenure.* San Francisco: Jossey-Bass, 1982.

Ehrenberg, R., Pieper P., and Willis, R. "Would Reducing Tenure Probabilities Increase Faculty Salaries? NBER Working Paper Series, no. 5150. Cambridge, Mass.: National Bureau of Economic Research, 1995.

Freidson, E. *Professionalism Reborn: Theory, Prophecy and Policy.* Chicago: University of Chicago Press, 1994.

Gappa, J. *Part-time Faculty: Higher Education at a Crossroads.* ASHE-ERIC Higher Education Research Report no. 3. Washington, D.C.: Association for the Study of Higher Education, 1984.

Gappa, J., and Leslie, D. *The Invisible Faculty.* San Francisco: Jossey-Bass, 1993.

Gemmill, J. "Course by Course, Year by Year. In M. E. Wallace (ed.), *Part-time Academic Employment.* New York: Modern Language Association, 1984.

Leslie, D., Kellams, S., and Gunne, G. M. *Part-time Faculty in American Higher Education.* New York: Praeger, 1982.

McPherson, M., and Winston, G. "The Economics of Academic Tenure: A Relational Perspective. In D. Breneman and T. Youn (eds.), *Academic Labor Markets and Careers.* New York: Falmer Press, 1988.

Pratt, L. "Disposable Faculty: Part-Time Exploitation as Management Strategy. In C. Nelson (ed.), *Will Teach for Food.* Minneapolis: University of Minnesota Press, 1997.

O'Toole, J., Van Alstyne, W., and Chait, R. *Tenure: Three Views.* New York: Change Magazine Press, 1979.

Rhoades, G. "Reorganizing the Faculty Workforce for Flexibility." *Journal of Higher Education,* 1996, *67* (6), 626–659.

South, S., Bonjean, C., Markham, W. T., and Corder, J. "Social Structure and Intergroup Interaction: Men and Women of the Federal Bureaucracy." *American Sociological Review,* 1982, *47* (3), 587–599.

Tolbert, P., Simons, T., and Andrews, A. "The Effects of Gender Composition in Academic Departments on Faculty Turnover." *Industrial and Labor Relations Review,* 1995, *48* (2), 562–579.

Tolbert, P. "Changing Employment Structures: The Case of Academia." Working paper, Department of Organizational Behavior, School of Industrial and Labor Relations, Cornell University, 1997.

PAMELA S. TOLBERT *is associate professor, Department of Organizational Behavior, New York School of Industrial and Labor Relations.*

A state university provost analyzes why his institution employs part-time faculty, discusses problems and solutions, and makes recommendations for longer-term policy development to assure quality education.

Part-Time Faculty, Quality Programs, and Economic Realities

John D. Haeger

The use of part-time faculty is again a major issue on college campuses across the nation. In reality, colleges and universities have used part-time faculty for years. In some institutions, such as Nova Southeastern University and the University of Phoenix, temporary faculty are the rule rather than the exception. What is new today is that part-time faculty are more vocal, more a fixture on four-year campuses, and more a solution to declining institutional budgets than ever before. There are also important—although neither fully articulated nor demonstrated—concerns that an excessive use of part-time faculty affects the quality of both undergraduate and graduate programs.

My purpose is to provide an overview of the characteristics of part-time faculty at Towson University, the reasons for their use, and the academic issues surrounding part-time faculty employment. I hope this case study will offer some insights that are applicable to other campuses.

Towson University is a large, comprehensive, metropolitan institution with 15,000 students; it is located on the northern border of Baltimore. The campus has approximately 2,100 graduate students in a student mix that is 25 percent residential and 75 percent commuter. Towson has been identified for growth by the University System of Maryland and expects to enroll in excess of 20,000 students by the year 2004. The faculty is composed of 478 tenured and tenure-track faculty and includes another 298 full-time equivalent (FTE) in part-time faculty. Within that 298 FTE are more than 400 individuals teaching from one to three courses per semester. The distribution of part-time faculty varies widely among departments, with higher proportions in art (61.5 percent of FTE faculty are part-time), psychology (58.6 percent), speech pathology and audiology (54.6 percent), music (51 percent), mass communication and communication studies (49.4 percent), mathematics (48.9 percent), sociology (47.7 percent), and English (45.9 percent). Equally notable are the departments that employ part-time faculty in much lower numbers: marketing (3.4 percent), accounting (26.3 percent), economics (28.3 percent), biology (30.7 percent), political science (32.2 percent), and management (35.8 percent).

Table 8.1 presents a historical view of part-time faculty levels university-wide over a twelve-year period, revealing the steady increase in the numbers and proportions in the late 1980s and early 1990s (from 21 percent in 1986 to 43 percent in 1997).

Rationale for Part-Time Faculty Use

What factors led to the increase in numbers of part-timers at Towson University?

Budgetary constraints. The single most important reason for this pattern was the tightness of the university's budget throughout the 1980s. Maryland's economy was in a major recession that lasted into the early 1990s. During several years the university was forced to return money to the state in the middle of the academic year. This resulted in several actions by the administration. First, there was a reluctance to fill positions opened up by resignations and retirements with new tenure-track faculty because of the unsettled budget. It was sound financial policy to fill tenure-track slots with part-time faculty and capture the salary savings. In some cases, positions were surrendered to the state as part of enrollment declines and budget tightening. Because contractual faculty receive only minimal benefits, each vacancy represented a potential $60,000 savings to the academic affairs budget.

Table 8.1. Trends in Proportion of Part-Time Faculty, 1986–1997

Fall, 19–	Budgeted	Adjusted	Part-Time	Proportion Part-Time
86	489	424.45	113.11	21.04%
87	489	413.03	112.25	21.40
88	506	429.99	136.47	24.10
89	540	464.34	192.33	29.30
90	538	444.87	194.81	29.70
91	528	429.65	201.46	31.90
92	517	419.48	226.28	35.00
93	517	401.25	234.7	36.90
94	507	401.58	243.05	37.70
95	489	397.3	252.75	38.9
96	488	393.38	264.87	40.30
97	490	393.13	298.09	43.10

Note: Assigned time, sabbaticals, and leaves not included.

Source: Data provided by Towson University.

Budget reduction through attrition. The university decided to reduce the budget through attrition rather than targeted reductions for reasons of quality or centrality to mission. In a time of fiscal stringency, the administration was unwilling to further fracture the sense of community by targeting specific departments for reduction. As a consequence, the reduction in FTE among departments was random. The art department can still name each of the five positions it lost. It received some part-time replacements, but these retirements left a gaping hole in the coverage of various fields. The physics and chemistry departments, although today very healthy in terms of enrollments, still have not recovered from the fact that they were targeted for closure by the University System of Maryland to reduce program duplication and to cut faculty positions.

Use of salary savings for operating funds. With tight budgets, the provost and deans realized that a portion of the dollars freed up from tenure lines could be applied to equipment purchases or departmental operating funds. Consequently, the university maintained its ability to run programs by cannibalizing the number of tenure-track lines. Over the five-year period, the number of filled tenure lines fell from 535 to 478. At the same time, the number of part-time FTE grew from 192 to 298. Equally important, enrollment had a one-year dip but then stabilized and now has, once again, shown signs of growth. These figures also reveal that even with stable and increasing enrollment, tenure-track lines remain on a decline and the part-time lines continue to increase.

Use of part-time faculty for flexibility. Once begun, the strategy of reducing tenure-track lines to provide budget flexibility developed a momentum of its own. The university constantly reiterated the need to maintain flexibility in departments, and the percentage of salary dollars committed to tenured lines was tightly controlled. I asked for a list of percentages of faculty who were tenured in departments and was shown figures of the percent of tenure-track to tenured lines; nearly every department was more than 85 percent tenured. In every department, though, there were so many part-time faculty that flexibility was assured.

I point out this example to show how institutional thinking is affected after years of deep budget cuts and constant attacks on programs. In effect, the reduction of tenured lines and the increase in part-time faculty had gained the status of institutional policy and had created a budget system that funded equipment and operating budgets by converting tenure lines.

Today we are reversing the process. Part-time money is being used to fund tenured lines; operating budgets and equipment are again being given identities of their own. However, it will take just as many years to recover as it did to create the problem. To create one hundred tenure-track lines from part-time positions is about a $4-million issue and can only be phased in over time.

Use of part-timers to vary programs. Hidden in these figures is our goal as a metropolitan university to use a number of part-time faculty who contribute to the ongoing quality of the academic programs. Many departments with a professional orientation actively seek part-time faculty who possess expertise not available on the current faculty. For example, the Department of Mass Communication and the Department of Communications Studies ask members of the local press, television, and radio industries to teach courses. In the College of Education, we try to establish strong partnerships with the K–12 districts, especially in Baltimore County. In the music and art departments, the Baltimore community has many professional artists and musicians who are highly sought after for their contributions to the programs. Our students benefit greatly from the expertise of the local business community in accounting, finance, the health professions, and technology. Thus, as a matter of academic policy and for reasons of concern for the students' real-world experiences, we seek to have a certain percentage of our faculty as part-time. The issue is always to find a valid and workable percentage that reinforces quality and benefits the students.

Identifying the Part-Time Faculty

Over the last three years, we have devoted considerable effort to understanding the characteristics of the part-time faculty at Towson University. We have conducted interviews and surveys of attitudes and concerns. Popular wisdom has been that part-time faculty are primarily women who teach one course periodically, that they have no continuing attachment to the university, and that they do not desire to serve on committees or advise as part of their role. Our part-time faculty are not unlike those reported in other forums. In the spring of 1996, 450 individuals taught one or more courses. Fifty-four percent were female, 20 percent held doctoral degrees, and 75 percent held a master's degree in the field of teaching. The majority taught only one course (56 percent), 101 (22 percent) taught two courses, and 60 (13 percent) taught three courses. Of the 450 faculty, nearly 90 percent had previous experience at Towson University. Indeed, one of the most remarkable characteristics of adjunct faculty is that many have fifteen and twenty years of experience at the university and feel a strong attachment to the institution and its students.

Over the last two years, the president and provost have regularly met with the part-time faculty. Through this vehicle, as well as through surveys, we gathered a litany of complaints from the part-time faculty about the university as a whole and about their respective departments. These complaints were primarily economic and related to compensation, but several other issues focused on quality programming. The most frequently mentioned adjunct faculty complaints that have emerged on our campus are as follows:

Lack of inclusion by most departments in meetings and committees, even when issues are directly relevant to part-time faculty, such as a course for which they are responsible
Absence of offices, telephones, support staff, and equipment
Lack of computer resources for classes and to communicate over the Internet
Inadequate compensation, lack of benefits, and untimely notification of teaching opportunities

No university guides or handbooks of services, expectations, calendar of dates, and student policies

No consideration for permanent appointment when an opportunity arises (holding a part-time appointment often seen as a negative)

Quality Issues

Across the country, concerns are expressed that the use of part-time faculty reduces the number and influence of tenure-track faculty. Will the lower compensation and episodic employment patterns destroy the professoriate as we know it? I think this worry is well founded. There seems little doubt that tenure or tenure-track contracts will no longer be the dominant form of employment within colleges and universities. Most institutions are moving to varied contracts—some tenured, some for a specific term, and some part-time appointments. For many universities, the real challenge is to recognize the economic and educational value of part-time faculty and then to develop policies that ensure that all appointments are part of the campus academic community.

The most important academic concern is the perception that part-time faculty threaten the quality of academic programs in terms of course content, advising, faculty-student interaction, and collegiality within academic departments.

On most campuses, particularly in metropolitan environments, part-time faculty, usually entry-level Ph.D.'s or those with master's degrees, bear large responsibility for general education courses. Departments prefer to use permanent faculty for majors in advanced-level course work. At Towson University, 45 percent of 885 sections of general education courses were handled by part-time faculty. For a campus that tells parents that their sons and daughters are taught by "real" faculty and not graduate assistants, one wonders if that statement needs clarification. There are also some interesting departmental variations in these patterns. In departments with large numbers of majors, such as biology, computer science, mathematics, and psychology or where student demand is high for reasons of fulfilling specific requirements, such as Spanish, the percentages are higher than average.

But is the percentage of part-time faculty involved in general education a quality issue? Teaching evaluations for these instructors are at the same level as tenured faculty. To my knowledge, no department or body of students has raised questions that the general level of competence of part-time instructors was an issue. Our statistics also show that part-time faculty are appropriately qualified for their assignments in terms of degrees and experience.

I would argue that the quality issues are less about what occurs in the classroom and more about the general environment that supports learning. Part-time faculty often do not have offices and therefore hold limited or no office hours. They do not have telephones on campus or must route all calls through a single line. They are not usually listed in the campus directory. Moreover, first- and second-year students, who are often the most in need of academic advice, must increasingly turn to faculty who have limited knowledge of the institution and its programs and who are not compensated for the time required to do advising.

The learning environment suffers most dramatically in terms of universitywide advising and committee work on curricular issues. In the first year I was at Towson University, I heard endless complaints from the faculty about their workloads; there were more students, and they could not get to all the papers and appointments with students. Yet every time I looked at the ratio of students to faculty, which lingers at around 1:17 and has not changed in ten years, I knew that student numbers alone were not the problem. The real issue was the increase in part-time faculty and the decrease in the number of permanent faculty to advise students, to serve on curricular committees, and to write grant proposals. By increasing part-time faculty, we reduced the number of faculty contributing to the general learning environment and to the shared governance of the institution.

Large numbers of part-time faculty who are paid less and have a nearly invisible role in the departments disrupts the departmental culture of teaching and research. Most departments do not understand the problems created by the use of part-time faculty and lack policies to ensure an integration into the culture. Ultimately this affects the learning community, as well as efforts at assessment and at interdisciplinary teaching and research. Large pieces of the curriculum lack coherence and integration because one cannot tell from semester to semester who might be teaching key courses and to what extent there is common agreement on a sequential approach to the major.

One of the most profound changes in the academy has been the utilization of technology, not just as a teaching methodology but as a tool fundamentally reshaping what we know and how we know it. Simultaneously, we are developing a part-time professoriate, more than 50 percent of the faculty in some departments, who do not have access to the technology or do not know how to use it within the context of Towson University. How much is the university willing to invest in these faculty who are now only loosely attached to the community?

Solutions

These are serious problems to which we must respond in a coherent fashion. I believe that response will significantly reshape the notion of university faculty. I am not naive enough to believe that metropolitan universities will suddenly stop using part-time faculty. Not only would the budget ramifications prevent such actions but most academic officers realize that part-time faculties contribute to the quality of academic programming. However, academic departments, colleges, and the Office of the Provost have to be more concerned about finding a systematic approach to structuring a part-time faculty culture that lessens the burdens on individuals and ensures adequate support for the learning environment. Although not a model, Towson University has taken steps to ensure a better learning environment for students and a more satisfying experience for the tenure-track and part-time faculty. The steps the university has taken include the following:

Establishing a series of lecturer appointments that have worked well for a few part-time faculty. Institutions should experiment with continuing appointments for some part-time faculty who teach for the institution year after year. The appointment could be full- or part-time and be given a "semipermanent" status both within the university and the department. These individuals could then have office space, telephones, and computer access.

Delegating overall responsibility for part-time faculty policies and communication to a person or office, in our case, the office of the provost. We now have a newsletter for part-time faculty; we have receptions that include the president, provost, deans, and chairs; invitations are sent to faculty about major university events; and an orientation program specifically designed for part-time faculty is presented each semester.

Recognizing that part-time faculty are an important element in the faculty mix and that changes must be made to the existing structures of faculty life. Change at Towson occurred in department membership, in advising, and in representation in the university senate. The universitywide advising systems must be rethought so that not all advising is dropped on full-time faculty, and more recognition is given advising as part of the promotion and tenure process for regular faculty.

Developing university guidelines for departments to ensure that part-time faculty can be successful in the classroom. What is the appropriate percentage of part-time faculty in the departments of mathematics, psychology, and mass communication? Each department should carefully orchestrate their use so that students receive the benefits of the expertise of the part-time faculty but do not lose contact with the regular faculty or access to advising and the disciplinary culture. In effect, departments must be far more systematic about how part-time faculty are used to ensure a good learning environment.

Conclusion

The reality is that part-time faculty are critical to the operation of the university. They unquestionably provide the economic base that allows the university to offer high-quality programs to an ever-increasing number of students. However, the university must control the negatives of part-time faculty employment and ensure support for the learning environment by placing part-time faculty in the mainstream of campus life. A real advantage of traditional colleges and universities competing with the University of Phoenix or electronically delivered programs is the continuing interaction between faculty and students. If we lose the feel and reality of an academic community and students and faculty pass like ships in the night, why would students continue to come to the university instead of selecting one of the cheaper alternatives?

JOHN D. HAEGER is provost and vice president for academic affairs, Towson University, Towson, Maryland.

Supporting adjunct faculty can make their teaching more effective.

Adjunct Faculty in the Community College: Realities and Challenges

Barbara A. Wyles

Higher education has become structurally dependent on part-time faculty. Over the last two decades, the percentage of teaching done by part-time faculty has increased to approximately 45 percent. In 1992, in all fifty states, the part-time faculty cohort equaled 55 to 65 percent of all community college faculty (Roueche, Roueche, and Milliron, 1995).

The community college's challenge—meeting escalating demands with declining resources—has resulted in spiraling increases in part-time faculty hiring. Such faculty are often hired to maintain close ties with business and industry; many are practitioners in the field in which they are teaching. That way, the college can remain on the cutting edge in the face of changing career needs, skill expectations, and the nature of work. Colleges are acutely aware that these same practitioners have strengthened the occupational and technical programs with the application of real-life perspectives. In addition, new skills-related technology courses often require expertise that full-time faculty do not have.

However, those who depend on part-time teaching for income or as entrée to a career face the reality of one-term contracts, median pay of $1,500 for a typical three-credit course (Avakian, 1995), a static pay scale, and only rare opportunities to convert their jobs into full-time appointments (making the foot-in-the-door promise an empty dream for most). In the end, part-time teaching experience translates into a red flag on a résumé that signals a suspicious pattern of temporary jobs.

The Landscape: A Systemic Picture

One-half of all current full-time community college faculty are expected to retire over the next five years. Coupled with decreased funding and the growing number of underprepared students, these projected retirements suggest that the demand for part-time faculty can only increase.

This situation for part-time faculty is simply a microcosm of our national economy in which one in three workers is a contingent worker. Nationally, from 1969 to 1992 the number of part-time workers has increased by 88.9 percent, and approximately 75 percent of new teaching jobs are filled by part-time faculty. Plagued with tax limits and competing demands for appropriated funds, many state and local governments have cut their workforces. Policymakers in some states have been willing to make access to higher education more difficult, and some educational institutions have raised admission standards in order to restrict enrollment to more highly qualified students. (Several board members of the State Council of Higher Education in Virginia have repeatedly voiced the opinion that "too many students are in college," and New York is grappling with the place of remedial education in the community colleges affiliated with City University.)

The shift to increasing the numbers of part-time hires is part of the wider employment pattern of downsizing, subcontracting, and outsourcing. In this respect, adjunct faculty can identify with the challenges and concerns of other, rather disparate groups (cafeteria workers, building and grounds employees, among others). At the same time, adjunct faculty have dispelled the old and outworn pronouncements that part-time faculty are less committed employees, less effective teachers, and less credentialed faculty. Evidence from my institution's experience shows that the current adjunct cohort receives student evaluations showing them to be as effective in the classroom as their full-time colleagues, that they have produced student outcomes that compete favorably with those of full-time faculty, and that they have earned credentials of equal status to their full-time counterparts.

In most institutions, however, part-time faculty are marginalized. They have no voice in curricular development, in textbook selection, in the work of their respective divisions, or generally, in the governance of the institution. The resulting credentialing without credibility, responsibility without authority, and expectations without rewards means that part-time faculty are asked to serve with loyalty and dedication without enjoying reciprocal trust and professional respect from their institutions. (Indeed, academia often fosters a conflict between the collective and the individual identity). A climate of job insecurity, vulnerability, and marginalization of an entire "class" results. The "Statement from the Conference on the Growing Use of Part-Time and Adjunct Faculty, September 26–28, 1997" (Statement, 1997) cites this dichotomy in dramatic terms: "A shrinking Brahmin class of professional-rank faculty enjoys academic careers and compensation commensurate with their advanced training, while a growing caste of 'untouchable' educational service workers are caught in poorly remunerated semester-to-semester jobs that offer no career prospects."

One Institution's Response

With a student population of nearly 63,000, located on five campuses, Northern Virginia Community College (NVCC) is the second-largest multicampus community college in the country. It is one of twenty-three community colleges in the Virginia Community College System and generates approximately one-third of the full-time equivalent student registrations for the system. Begun in 1965 and chartered as a technical college, its identity and attendant mission soon defined it as a community college. As such, it offers both transfer and occupational technical degree programs, as well as developmental education and continuing education. Increasingly, its mission has come to include economic development through delivery of education and training to business, industry, and government. Collegewide, there are 500 full-time and approximately 1,100 part-time faculty, with part-time faculty representing approximately 68.75 percent of the faculty.

The Alexandria campus is the second largest of the five campuses of Northern Virginia Community College, serving 11,340 students through 123 degree and certificate programs. It is by far the most diverse campus culturally; its student body represents 134 different countries, and its overall student population is approximately 52 percent minority and international. Full-time faculty number 179, and its adjunct cohort is approximately 325.

The college's largely urban setting presents many advantages (and recently a marked disadvantage) to the recruitment, hiring, and retention of qualified part-time faculty from a wide array of occupations. These are generally highly credentialed faculty with much sought-after expertise. Only recently has this benefit yielded to a "conflict of goods." High-end technological skills have been readily available in the community of workers and therefore of potential adjunct hires. Concomitant salaries for these skills have been forthcoming from business and industry, making these skilled workers busier and less "hungry." As a result, they are less available and less interested in part-time teaching.

One Campus's Policies and Practices. The task of recruiting and hiring part-time faculty is decentralized at NVCC. Although collegewide policy governs the requisite credentials for these hires, as well as promotion and pay scales, individual campuses establish practices by which adjunct faculty are identified, hired, scheduled, and evaluated. College policy limits credits taught per semester and per year by an adjunct faculty to nine and nineteen, respectively.

Some of the practices implemented at the Alexandria campus include the following:

An orientation session for all new adjuncts and returning adjuncts, along with full-time faculty, is scheduled for evening hours to avoid conflicts with the work schedules of those who work in other jobs during the day. The orientation sessions are organized by divisions, so faculty are grouped by teaching discipline.

A Saturday orientation for adjunct faculty begins with general information on the college and the campus, with more specific information provided at the division meetings that follow. The Saturday orientation generally includes a keynote speaker selected from the adjunct faculty, a question-and-answer discussion, and a panel or open discussion on relevant academic or instructional issues.

An end-of-year recognition for the campus's outstanding adjunct faculty. This practice is part of the end-of-year awards ceremony that gives special recognition to those who have been nominated and then selected by their peers to receive the awards for outstanding adjunct faculty, full-time faculty, administrator, and classified staff member.

A representative from the adjunct faculty body sits on the campus council, a policy-advisory body to the college senate.

In 1996–97, the first adjunct faculty member took part in an exchange with the Cheshire Education Management Programme in England. The exchange takes place for two weeks in October, with an identified partner from England, Northern Ireland, or Wales visiting the faculty exchange member at NVCC, and two weeks in May, when the NVCC faculty member visits the exchange faculty member's institution. This year, an adjunct faculty member was selected for an exchange with a full-time faculty member from England.

Adjunct faculty take part in grant writing and grant directing.

On occasion, the names of "permanent part-time" faculty are listed in the schedule of classes.

The college has published a handbook entitled "Adjunct Faculty Handbook."

Problems and Issues

The overarching problem is not the growing number or the overall proportion of adjunct faculty; rather, it is the institutional neglect of this critical mass— not so much their neglect as their exclusion from the teaching-learning enterprise. They are disconnected from the community of learners; they lack sovereignty as a "collectivity" over the educational process; they are alienated from academic decision making and from the collegial process (McGuire, 1993).

Part-time faculty will continue to be "faculty of convenience" because they allow staffing of new courses driven by market demand, because they constitute a risk-free talent pool on which institutions rely for pilot programs to test student markets, and because they allow flexibility of scheduling at relatively low cost. Part-time faculty mirror dramatic changes in the wider world of work, in which there are fewer definitive jobs and more temporary "work situations." In these ways, higher education has come to depend on part-time faculty to reinvent itself in a time of great change. We cannot afford to marginalize such an important part of our faculty.

Integrating adjunct faculty into the culture of the learning organization therefore becomes a critical goal for higher education institutions. Toward this end, various assumptions about how we employ adjunct faculty need to be examined. These include

- Practices by which institutions recruit, select, and hire them
- Provisions of appointment and reappointment
- Establishment of appropriate working conditions

- Orientation to the institutional culture as well as orientation to policies and practices
- Integration into collegial campus and departmental processes
- Provision of professional development opportunities
- Evaluation of work consistent with responsibilities
- Establishment of equitable pay (as opposed to equal pay)

References

Avakian, N. A. "Conflicting Demands for Adjunct Faculty." *Community College Journal,* June/July 1995, 34–36.

McGuire, J. "Part-Time Faculty: Partners in Excellence." *Leadership Abstracts,* June 1993, 6 (6), 2–3 (ED 367 429).

Roueche, J. E., Roueche, S. D., and Milliron, M. D. *Strangers in Their Own Land.* Washington, D.C.: Community College Press, 1995.

Statement from the Conference on the Growing Use of Part-Time and Adjunct Faculty, Sept. 26–28, 1997. *Academe Today*: Document Archive, Dec. 1, 1997.

BARBARA A. WYLES is provost of the Alexandria campus of Northern Virginia Community College, Alexandria, Virginia.

The contributions to this volume point to issues for research, policy development, and improving practice.

New Directions for Research, Policy Development, and Practice

David W. Leslie

The Sloan Conference on Part-Time and Adjunct Faculty brought scholars from varied disciplines together to share research, perspectives, and ideas about important changes taking place in academic employment. Participants explored causes, effects, and implications of a dramatic shift from full-time to part-time jobs. Conferees acknowledged that the use of part-time and adjunct faculty is a multivariate phenomenon. It has varied roots, varied manifestations, and varied effects—from discipline to discipline, from institution to institution, and from one type of institution (research universities, for example) to another type of institution (community colleges, for example).

As higher education has expanded—taking on new missions and programs, serving new populations, and adding capacity with new and larger community colleges—so too is the definition of *faculty* beginning to change. As Langenberg's chapter marking the *subfaculty* as a growing part of the academic workforce implies, and as Tolbert's analysis of departmental mitosis illustrates, faculty work and faculty roles may be evolving through a sort of vertical differentiation.

But constraints on funding for higher education, shifting patterns in jobs and careers, and misalignment of supply and demand have dislocated academic employment patterns, too. Institutions have found themselves teaching more students with less money. Student enrollment has shifted, and new disciplines and professions have emerged to put heavier demands for specialized faculty on college and university budgets.

Faculty employment patterns have become markedly different among the varied teaching fields as well (Clark, 1997). Sloan Conference participants noted that these emerging patterns may have overrun the traditional faculty career patterns, leaving them characteristic only of the minority of all who teach in higher education. The new majority of faculty do more varied work, in more varied settings, on more varied terms and conditions—and bring more varied preparation and qualifications to academic life.

This realization prompted concerns about the viability and appeal of traditional faculty careers and about the traditional tenure system as an underpinning for quality in teaching, research, and service. It also moved Sloan Conference participants to raise important questions for research, and about existing policies and practices.

Research Issues. Current understanding about the use of part-time and adjunct faculty has been advanced to a great degree by the availability of data from the National Survey of Postsecondary Faculty conducted by the National Center for Education Statistics in 1992. This was easily the largest national survey of its kind ever undertaken and easily the most representative of part-time and adjunct faculty. The data from that survey were gathered (at this writing) nearly six years ago—six years in which change has gone largely unmonitored. Although a new survey is due to be distributed in the fall of 1998, publication of the results will lag, perhaps by years. One of the principal needs is a *more continuous way to monitor trends* in faculty work and employment patterns so that there will be no long gaps in the available data.

The other principal issue in analyzing faculty work, jobs, and careers is to find the *appropriate level of disaggregation.* Issues related to part-time and adjunct faculty appear to be highly specific to individual disciplines and to the different types of institutions. English, the foreign languages, and the fine arts, for example, appear to face distinct issues relating to the division of labor, supply and demand, career prospects, and morale. Health professions, business, and law employ substantial numbers of part-time faculty, but the issues in those fields appear much different, particularly because highly paid employment outside academe is available. Although the popular literature suggests widespread exploitation, low morale, and a closing off of academic career prospects, those conditions are mainly concentrated in a few disciplines; quite different conditions characterize others. So one obvious need is to study part-time academic work within specific disciplines.

The second important distinction runs along the lines of the different institutional strata. Sixty percent of community college faculty are part-time. This sector is clearly in a far different situation than the research university sector, where just under one-quarter (23 percent) of the faculty are part-time. However, research universities show a greater degree of vertical specialization in the distribution of work and in the differentiation of jobs. Not only is teaching the largest (by far) component of faculty work in community colleges but it is concentrated at the lower division of undergraduate studies and is dispersed across a wide range of subjects, many of which are vocational in content. This context for faculty work, jobs, and careers is far different here than in research universities. The differences among these varied institutional settings are as great as among the settings in which medicine is practiced—from the walk-in clinics of rural areas to the hyper-sophisticated tertiary care research hospitals in the great cities. One can no more generalize about faculty than about doctors.

The availability of large amounts of data from the NCES surveys will be helpful in pursuing disaggregated analyses of faculty work and careers, but field-based qualitative studies may be even more fruitful in yielding up more textured and grounded understandings about who faculty are, what they do, and how their work lives are connected to and play out in varied institutional and disciplinary contexts.

Policy Issues. The Sloan Conference participants recognized that the supply of and demand for faculty are asynchronous in some fields. Although the overall production of doctorates has shown a steady increase, the quality of preparation for faculty work by those completing doctorates, the distribution of degrees over the many disciplines, and the stages of entry into research, teaching, and service strands of the academic career are problematic.

Production of doctorates is, of course, a joint result of federal, state, and institutional policy. It is also very much a product of the intellectual gatekeeping function of the organized disciplines. The Commission on Professionals in Science and Technology produced a study of the postdoctoral experience in 1997. The issues addressed in that report are highly relevant to analysis of all non-tenure-track faculty employment, as well as to questions about career entry, socialization, and advancement. The CPST report suggests (directly or indirectly) that questions such as these need to be addressed:

What is the level of risk perceived by prospective doctoral students as they commit to advanced degree studies and to preparation for academic careers? (Will "real" jobs be available at the end of the long tunnel?)

What are the disincentives facing prospective faculty? How can they maximize their chances of going from beginning graduate student to tenured faculty member? How manageable are the career hurdles, and how good will their jobs be when they finish?

How well are the conditions of work for prospective faculty known? How thoroughly are they monitored? Given that postdoctoral appointments, part-time or adjunct teaching, and research appointments serve as holding patterns for many prospective faculty, are the terms of employment sufficient to keep the best and brightest prospects productively engaged and well-prepared for entry? Are these positions being overused or becoming exploitive of a large surplus of doctoral graduates?

Who should fund the queued up, but underemployed, doctorate-holders? Is there a larger national interest in helping to sustain this talent pool through their search for work? Or are they to be left to their own resources?

How can academic employment be made sufficiently attractive in competition with nonacademic alternatives that are abundantly available to Ph.D.'s in many fields? Although intrinsic motivation to teach and do research holds many new doctoral graduates in the pipeline, many of them will have to calculate their economic interests against alternative employment prospects. (Can they make big money now instead of gambling on the pipeline that allocates the most desirable academic jobs—a pipeline that is very crowded in some fields?)

More immediate policy issues confront institutions that employ large numbers of part-time faculty (Gappa and Leslie, 1993). Part-time and adjunct faculty do much of the core production (undergraduate teaching) in many departments, and very nearly all of it in some. Individual part-time or adjunct faculty are often long-term employees who have accumulated experience and exercise considerable discretion and control over courses and programs. Yet they are often denied a substantive role in academic governance, curriculum development, faculty hiring, and related decision processes that intimately affect their own work and the broader qualitative dimensions of the academic programs in which they teach.

How integral a role should part-time and adjunct faculty play in the life of the academic community? If faculty work is as interrelated as theory suggests (for example, teaching for common outcomes of liberal education), can that work be effective when status and political divisions between full partners and contingent contract workers are reinforced by exclusive access to decision making for only one group?

A related question concerns the investment that institutions make in human capacity. If part-time and adjunct faculty are seen as a stop-gap for temporary needs, will institutions invest in their development as effective faculty? Evidence shows that part-timers, on average, stay in these jobs for considerable periods of time. If they return value commensurate with their experience, commitment, morale, and expertise, shouldn't institutions invest in assuring such a return?

Perhaps more globally, the dramatic increase in level of part-time employment at colleges and universities, apparently well beyond the level of contingent work in the broader economy, raises serious questions about the health of the academic enterprise. We know very little about how organizations that rely principally on temporary employees (for example, community colleges in which as many as 80 percent of faculty are part-time) cope with their own basic survival tasks. Can they build strong internal cultures, do effective work, serve their clients, maintain continuity, and adapt to changing environments?

In addition to these basic tasks, academic organizations thrive on the individual creativity and intellectual freedom of their faculty. These qualities are protected and sustained through policies on academic freedom and tenure. Current trends appear to show that fewer than half of all faculty are eligible for tenure. Does the new majority of part-time and temporary faculty enjoy equal protection for their academic freedom? Because the academic community's main value to society is the unfettered search for truth, the consequences if they are not protected could be serious for the attractiveness of academic careers, for the social processes of discovery and creation, and for the viability of colleges and universities as legitimate social institutions.

Implications for Practice

In *The Invisible Faculty,* Gappa and Leslie (1993) point out that the number or proportion of part-time faculty is less important than the practices that ensure quality in delivering education. They recommended attention to three areas: (1) achieving educational objectives, (2) being fair in employment practice, and (3) investing in human resources.

They found that using part-time faculty to save money instead of to serve some academic purpose had a negative impact on quality. When part-time faculty are hired because they will work for low pay rather than because they are the best-qualified candidates, high-quality educational results are less likely. (Gappa and Leslie, 1997).

A second major problem lies in capricious and unfair treatment of part-time faculty. Part-time faculty are often hired at the last minute, paid low and arbitrarily varying rates, denied access to benefits, and subjected to limits on the amount and kind of work they are assigned. They are also routinely terminated when the continuity of their employment approaches the minimum required for vesting in various benefits and other protections. Part-time faculty powerfully resent the inequities they endure, and inequitable treatment often affects their morale and their commitment.

Third, part-time faculty often work without the normal support services that full-time faculty take for granted. For example, offices, telephones, computers, secretarial and other administrative support, and professional development funds provide the infrastructure that undergirds competent and effective teaching. Stories of part-time faculty trying to counsel students in their cars or having trouble getting materials from the library or having no computers are common in the popular lore. Full-time faculty simply would not work under the same conditions. Part-time faculty clearly cannot be expected to develop their skills and their expertise unless institutions make serious investments in the infrastructure that enables them to grow and improve.

Conclusion

Part-time and adjunct faculty may bring added value to the institutions in which they teach, and they may teach for the best of reasons and with the strongest of capabilities. But they often do so under conditions that belie their employing institutions' commitment to quality instruction, to the long-term pursuit of substantive research, or to their standing as exemplary intellectual communities. They also take great personal risks in many cases, hoping for years that they might achieve full membership in the academic profession but becoming progressively disillusioned and marginalized by the realities they experience. These realities, confronted honestly, pose serious dilemmas for those institutions that rely heavily on part-time and adjunct faculty—dilemmas of ethics, dilemmas of policy, and dilemmas in practice.

But the overriding concern of the Sloan Conference participants was the need for more penetrating understanding of the academic workforce, academic workplace, academic career, and academic profession. Who will be attracted to professional scholarship? What will it cost them (and the nation) to prepare? What kinds of jobs and what kinds of rewards will sustain them?

How will their work be divided up? Who will teach, who will discover, who will apply knowledge, who will serve? The comforting paradigm of a tenured and tenurable faculty is challenged by an emerging understanding that college and university teaching is no longer a stable career prospect. It is becoming, more and more, just a job, and a temporary one at that. How and why that is happening, and what its effects are, remains a subject for serious and sustained inquiry.

References

Clark, B. R. "Small Worlds, Different Worlds: The Uniquenesses and Troubles of American Academic Professions." *Daedalus*, 1997, *126* (4), 21–42.

Commission on Professionals in Science and Technology. *Postdocs and Career Prospects: A Status Report.* Washington, D.C.: Commission on Professionals in Science and Technology, 1997.

J. M. Gappa, and D. W. Leslie. *The Invisible Faculty.* San Francisco: Jossey-Bass, 1993.

DAVID W. LESLIE is professor of education at the College of William and Mary, Williamsburg, Virginia.

Index

Academic careers: advancement and entry to, 67, 89, 97; business and industry or, 62–63; framework for assessing trends in, 19–27; influences on, 21–27; instability of, 62–63, 100; and job status issues, 43–44, 66; job uncertainty trend in, 63–67; normative aspects of, 20, 23, 24; pervasive changes affecting, 24–27; in S&E fields, 62–63; and specific higher education practices, 22; structural aspects of, 20, 21, 23, 25, 26; as temporary jobs, 89, 100; theoretical dimensions of, 19–21; work and the idea of, 2. *See also* Employment patterns, faculty; Tracks, employment

Academic department policies toward part-time faculty: and attrition, 83; case study, 72–74; hiring decisions, 13, 73; organizational implications of, 76–78; strategies for, 15, 67–68, 74–76, 86–87. *See also* Employment practice, academic

Academic work patterns. *See* Workforce, the academic

Accessibility to students, faculty, 13–14, 15, 17, 23, 57, 58, 87

Adjunct faculty, definition of, 1, 40–41. *See also* Nontraditional faculty; Part-time faculty

Administrators: justification of policies by, 14, 77–78; responsibility for part-time faculty, 87. *See also* Hiring of part-time faculty

Advisors, faculty, 65, 67, 85–86, 87

Affirmative action, 24

Alexandria campus, NVCC, 91–92

Alfred P. Sloan Foundation, 1, 2, 99–100

American Association of University Professors, 79

Andrews, A., 78

Angus, I., 16

Appelbaum, E., 38

Association of American Universities, 64

Astin, A. W., 61

Attitudes: of students, 42–43, 66; of tenured faculty, 73–74, 77. *See also* Part-time faculty

Attrition, budget reduction through, 83

Avakian, N. A., 89

Awards, faculty earning undergraduate, 52–53

Aylesworth, K., 64

Baby-boom cohort, 17

Backburn, R., 20

Baldwin, R. G., 4

Bean, J. P., 24

Benefits and pensions, 34, 35, 36, 50, 51, 74

Benjamin, E., 59

Bernstein, J., 32

Berver, K., 71

Bianco-Mathis, V., 71

Biles, G., 71

Biles, G. E., 13, 16

Blackburn, R., 19, 20, 23

Blue collar workers, 33

Bonjean, C., 78

Boyer, E., 23

Brown, P., 66

Bureau of Labor Statistics (BLS), 30, 31

Business faculty, 46, 47

Business, jobs in, 62–63, 91

Career and career course, 19. *See also* Academic careers

Case studies: part-time faculty, 81–87; two-tiered faculty, 72–76

Cassirer, N., 33

Chait, R., 78

Chalofsky, N., 71

Chronister, J. L., 4

Chubin, D. E., 64

Clark, B., 26

Clarke, J. E., 61, 63

Clinical faculty, 11, 12, 25

College or school policies toward part-time faculty: strategies and recommendations for, 12, 15–16, 67–68, 76–78, 86–87

Collegiality. *See* Culture, institutional; Full-time and part-time faculty

Commission on Professionals in Science and Technology, 67, 68, 97

Community, academic: political divisions, 98; status divisions, 43–44, 62, 98. *See also* Culture, institutional

Back Issue/Subscription Order Form

Copy or detach and send to:
Jossey-Bass Inc., Publishers, 350 Sansome Street, San Francisco CA 94104-1342

Call or fax toll free!
Phone 888-378-2537 6AM-5PM PST; Fax 800-605-2665

Back issues: Please send me the following issues at $23 each.
(Important: please include series initials and issue number, such as HE90.)

1. HE _____

_____

_____

$ _____ Total for single issues

$ _____ Shipping charges (for single issues *only;* subscriptions are exempt from shipping charges): Up to $30, add $5^{50} • $30^{01}–$50, add $6^{50} $50^{01}–$75, add $7^{50} • $75^{01}–$100, add $9 • $100^{01}–$150, add $10 Over $150, call for shipping charge.

Subscriptions Please ❑ start ❑ renew my subscription to *New Directions for Higher Education* for the year 19___ at the following rate:

❑ Individual $56   ❑ Institutional $99
NOTE: Subscriptions are quarterly, and are for the calendar year only. Subscriptions begin with the spring issue of the year indicated above. For shipping outside the U.S., please add $25.

$ _____ Total single issues and subscriptions (CA, IN, NJ, NY and DC residents, add sales tax for single issues. NY and DC residents must include shipping charges when calculating sales tax. NY and Canadian residents only, add sales tax for subscriptions.)

❑ Payment enclosed (U.S. check or money order only)
❑ VISA, MC, AmEx, Discover Card #_____ Exp. date_____

Signature _____ Day phone _____
❑ Bill me (U.S. institutional orders only. Purchase order required.)
Purchase order #_____

Name _____
Address _____

_____

Phone_____ E-mail _____

For more information about Jossey-Bass Publishers, visit our Web site at:
www.josseybass.com   **PRIORITY CODE = ND1**

UNITED STATES POSTAL SERVICE™

Statement of Ownership, Management, and Circulation
(Required by 39 USC 3685)

1. Publication Title	2. Publication Number	3. Filing Date
NEW DIRECTIONS FOR HIGHER EDUCATION	0 2 7 1 _ 0 5 6 0	10/14/98

4. Issue Frequency	5. Number of Issues Published Annually	6. Annual Subscription Price
QUARTERLY	4	$56 - indiv. $99 - instit.

7. Complete Mailing Address of Known Office of Publication *(Not printer) (Street, city, county, state, and ZIP+4)*	Contact Person
350 SANSOME STREET SAN FRANCISCO, CA 94104 (SAN FRANCISCO COUNTY)	ROGER HUNT
	Telephone
	415 782 3232

8. Complete Mailing Address of Headquarters or General Business Office of Publisher *(Not printer)*

SAME AS ABOVE

9. Full Names and Complete Mailing Addresses of Publisher, Editor, and Managing Editor *(Do not leave blank)*

Publisher *(Name and complete mailing address)*

JOSSEY-BASS INC., PUBLISHERS
(ABOVE ADDRESS)

Editor *(Name and complete mailing address)*

MARTIN KRAMER
2807 SHASTA ROAD
BERKELEY, CA   94708-2011

Managing Editor *(Name and complete mailing address)*

NONE

10. Owner *(Do not leave blank. If the publication is owned by a corporation, give the name and address of the corporation immediately followed by the names and addresses of all stockholders owning or holding 1 percent or more of the total amount of stock. If not owned by a corporation, give the names and addresses of the individual owners. If owned by a partnership or other unincorporated firm, give its name and address as well as those of each individual owner. If the publication is published by a nonprofit organization, give its name and address.)*

Full Name	Complete Mailing Address
SIMON & SCHUSTER, INC.	P.O. BOX 1172
	ENGLEWOOD CLIFFS, NJ 07632-1172

11. Known Bondholders, Mortgagees, and Other Security Holders Owning or Holding 1 Percent or More of Total Amount of Bonds, Mortgages, or Other Securities. If none, check box ———▶ ☐ None

Full Name	Complete Mailing Address
SAME AS ABOVE	SAME AS ABOVE

12. Tax Status *(For completion by nonprofit organizations authorized to mail at special rates) (Check one)*
The purpose, function, and nonprofit status of this organization and the exempt status for federal income tax purposes:
☐ Has Not Changed During Preceding 12 Months
☐ Has Changed During Preceding 12 Months *(Publisher must submit explanation of change with this statement)*

PS Form **3526**, September 1995 *(See Instructions on Reverse)*

13. Publication Title	14. Issue Date for Circulation Data Below
NEW DIRECTIONS FOR HIGHER EDUCATION	FALL 1998

15.	Extent and Nature of Circulation	Average No. Copies Each Issue During Preceding 12 Months	Actual No. Copies of Single Issue Published Nearest to Filing Date
a. Total Number of Copies *(Net press run)*		1820	1843
b. Paid and/or Requested Circulation	(1) Sales Through Dealers and Carriers, Street Vendors, and Counter Sales *(Not mailed)*	158	29
	(2) Paid or Requested Mail Subscriptions *(Include advertiser's proof copies and exchange copies)*	864	884
c. Total Paid and/or Requested Circulation *(Sum of 15b(1) and 15b(2))* ▶		1022	913
d. Free Distribution by Mail *(Samples, complimentary, and other free)*		0	0
e. Free Distribution Outside the Mail *(Carriers or other means)*		239	173
f. Total Free Distribution *(Sum of 15d and 15e)* ▶		239	173
g. Total Distribution *(Sum of 15c and 15f)* ▶		1261	1086
h. Copies not Distributed	(1) Office Use, Leftovers, Spoiled	559	757
	(2) Returns from News Agents	0	0
i. Total *(Sum of 15g, 15h(1), and 15h(2))* ▶		1820	1843
Percent Paid and/or Requested Circulation *(15c / 15g x 100)*		81%	84%

16. Publication of Statement of Ownership
XX Publication required. Will be printed in the WINTER 1998 issue of this publication.
☐ Publication not required.

17. Signature and Title of Editor, Publisher, Business Manager, or Owner	Date
Susan E. Lewis SUSAN E. LEWIS PERIODICALS DIRECTOR	10/14/98

I certify that all information furnished on this form is true and complete. I understand that anyone who furnishes false or misleading information on this form or who omits material or information requested on the form may be subject to criminal sanctions (including fines and imprisonment) and/or civil sanctions (including multiple damages and civil penalties).

Instructions to Publishers

1. Complete and file one copy of this form with your postmaster annually on or before October 1. Keep a copy of the completed form for your records.

2. In cases where the stockholder or security holder is a trustee, include in items 10 and 11 the name of the person or corporation for whom the trustee is acting. Also include the names and addresses of individuals who are stockholders who own or hold 1 percent or more of the total amount of bonds, mortgages, or other securities of the publishing corporation. In item 11, if none, check the box. Use blank sheets if more space is required.

3. Be sure to furnish all circulation information called for in item 15. Free circulation must be shown in items 15d, e, and f.

4. If the publication had second-class authorization as a general or requester publication, this Statement of Ownership, Management, and Circulation must be published; it must be printed in any issue in October or, if the publication is not published during October, the first issue printed after October.

5. In item 16, indicate the date of the issue in which this Statement of Ownership will be published.

6. Item 17 must be signed.

Failure to file or publish a statement of ownership may lead to suspension of second-class authorization.

PS Form **3526**, September 1995 *(Reverse)*